C000261956

One-Pot Vegan Cookbook

One-Pot
VEGAN
COOKBOOK

125 Recipes for Your Dutch Oven, Sheet Pan, Electric Pressure Cooker, and More

Gunjan Dudani

Photography by Nadine Greeff

ROCKRIDGE PRESS

Copyright © 2020 by Rockridge Press, Emeryville, California

No part of this publication may be reproduced, stored in a retrieval system, or transmitted in any form or by any means, electronic, mechanical, photocopying, recording, scanning, or otherwise, except as permitted under Sections 107 or 108 of the 1976 United States Copyright Act, without the prior written permission of the Publisher. Requests to the Publisher for permission should be addressed to the Permissions Department, Rockridge Press, 6005 Shellmound Street, Suite 175, Emeryville, CA 94608.

Limit of Liability/Disclaimer of Warranty: The Publisher and the author make no representations or warranties with respect to the accuracy or completeness of the contents of this work and specifically disclaim all warranties, including without limitation warranties of fitness for a particular purpose. No warranty may be created or extended by sales or promotional materials. The advice and strategies contained herein may not be suitable for every situation. This work is sold with the understanding that the Publisher is not engaged in rendering medical, legal, or other professional advice or services. If professional assistance is required, the services of a competent professional person should be sought. Neither the Publisher nor the author shall be liable for damages arising herefrom. The fact that an individual, organization, or website is referred to in this work as a citation and/or potential source of further information does not mean that the author or the Publisher endorses the information the individual, organization, or website may provide or recommendations they/it may make. Further, readers should be aware that websites listed in this work may have changed or disappeared between when this work was written and when it is read.

For general information on our other products and services or to obtain technical support, please contact our Customer Care Department within the United States at (866) 744-2665, or outside the United States at (510) 253-0500.

Rockridge Press publishes its books in a variety of electronic and print formats. Some content that appears in print may not be available in electronic books, and vice versa.

TRADEMARKS: Rockridge Press and the Rockridge Press logo are trademarks or registered trademarks of Callisto Media Inc. and/or its affiliates, in the United States and other countries, and may not be used without written permission. All other trademarks are the property of their respective owners. Rockridge Press is not associated with any product or vendor mentioned in this book.

Interior & Cover Designer: Julie Gueraseva
Art Producer: Janice Ackerman
Editor: Adrian Potts
Production Editor: Matt Burnett
Photography: © 2020 Nadine Greeff
Cover: Spicy Shakshuka with Tofu, page 21

ISBN: Print 978-1-64611-656-0 | eBook 978-1-64611-657-7
R0

To my daughters, Yashvi and Ruvanshi,
who inspired me to take up cooking seriously

Contents

Introduction

As a busy mom of two beautiful girls, I know the difficulties of cooking vegan meals every day. For years, I struggled to figure out a healthy way to cook and eat while maintaining a balanced lifestyle. I often ended up ordering takeaway or dining out and, as a result, saw the scales and my blood pressure go up.

To embrace a healthier lifestyle I endeavored to cook more at home, and I explored the great potential of one-pot meals. Whether using a skillet, stockpot, electric pressure cooker, or slow cooker, I quickly noticed the benefits of using natural, flavorful ingredients while also spending less time in the kitchen.

With one-pot meals, everyday cooking has become so much easier because all I have to do is throw the ingredients in a pot and let them cook until they are done. Gone are the numerous vessels and appliances I once wielded, and there is almost no mess to clean up after.

Now we only order takeaway or eat out on special occasions, which also helps keep our family budget in check. I also have the opportunity to set an example of healthy eating habits for my kids. In terms of my own health and lifestyle, I have finally found a balance between maintaining a wholesome diet and spending quality time with my precious family. My one and only secret is one-pot cooking.

As a vegan, I'm aware it can sometimes be hard to find easy one-pot recipes that use familiar and affordable ingredients. With this book, I want to share the cost-effective recipes I have devised for my loved ones, using easily available ingredients. You don't have to be an expert cook to make these meals, nor do you need to spend hours in the kitchen. I have kept things simple and easy, yet each recipe is full of flavor so even your vegetarian and omnivore friends and family will be pleased.

I hope that through this book you enjoy healthier and tastier one-pot vegan meals in your own home.

Tofu Ramen Bowl,
page 35

Chapter 1

Easy One-Pot Vegan Cooking

After an exhausting day at work or out and about, the last thing you want to do is spend forever chopping, cooking, and cleaning up. Nor do you want to fuss around searching for and preparing specialty ingredients. Although there is a common misconception that vegan cooking requires more time and effort, I know firsthand it can be simple, easy, and delicious.

In this chapter, I introduce you to the basics of vegan one-pot cooking, including how to ensure your dietary needs are met, which types of cooking vessels you can use, and how to stock your kitchen with all the basics you'll need to make the recipes in this book.

One-Pot Cooking

When I say, "one-pot cooking," I really mean "one pot." You may need bowls to whisk or marinate ingredients, but otherwise all recipes in this book each use a single cooking vessel.

For variety, I have included a range of vessel types. Each is perfect for weeknight cooking as prep time is minimal and cooking everything together means you'll have fewer things waiting for you in the sink when you're done.

SKILLET

Skillets are ideal for frying, sautéing, and searing. Cast iron skillets are best and can be used on the stovetop and in the oven. A bigger skillet will hold all the ingredients for one-pot cooking.

STOCKPOT

A deep pot with long sides, stockpots are great for cooking broth and liquids. I use an 8-quart stockpot for my recipes, but you may use any size you have, depending on your servings.

DUTCH OVEN

A large, heavy enamel-coated cast iron pot that conducts and retains heat evenly, Dutch ovens are suitable for stovetop and oven cooking.

SHEET PAN

A type of baking sheet, a sheet pan is a flat metal pan, usually with rimmed sides, that's perfect for fuss-free oven cooking. A regular baking sheet is flat with no rimmed sides.

ELECTRIC PRESSURE COOKER

Pressure cookers allow you to cook foods that usually take a long time in record speed. I use a 6-quart cooker for my recipes.

SLOW COOKER

Also known as a crockpot, like the electric pressure cooker, this is another countertop electric appliance. The long cook times used allow ingredients to cook and marinate together with minimal attention for deliciously tender results.

AIR FRYER

Air fryers use a convection mechanism to circulate hot air around food without using tons of oil to cook it. This way, you enjoy the taste and texture of deep-fried food but in a healthier form. I use a 5.8-quart air fryer for my recipes and cook them in batches, but you may find a larger size to accommodate your food in one batch, depending on your needs.

Vegan Eating

When many people imagine a vegan diet, they tend to think of complicated recipes with healthy but bland ingredients. And, although plant-based eating is highly nutritious, it can and should be flavorful and fun!

Vegan cooking features the tastes and textures of naturally delicious vegetables, fruits, legumes, grains, nuts, and seeds. It also encourages you to be creative with flavorings, adding interesting twists with spices and seasonings, to serve some amazingly delicious and wholesome meals.

Adopting a plant-based diet doesn't mean you need to say goodbye to your favorite comfort foods. With a bit of ingenuity, you can enjoy the familiar flavors of non-vegan eating with the use of substitute ingredients.

BENEFITS OF A PLANT-BASED DIET

With rising levels of obesity, high cholesterol, heart disease, and many other chronic diseases in the United States, the plant-based diet has gained a lot of attention recently. With a focus on natural wholesome ingredients, this type of eating comes with bountiful health benefits.

Research published in *Permanente Journal* found that a diet embracing plant-based foods and discouraging meat and dairy products and refined and processed foods is effective in reducing the risk of obesity, diabetes, and cardiovascular disease.

By adopting a plant-based diet, you are cutting out refined sugars and saturated fats prevalent in packaged and fast foods, while enjoying ingredients rich in antioxidants, vitamins, and minerals. A plant-based diet also provides plenty of fiber, which, according to a study in the journal *Nutrition*, is associated with a healthy body weight and body fat levels.

And, according to the American Institute of Cancer Research, foods low in calories and high in fiber help fight and prevent cancer. They recommend filling at least two-thirds of your plate with plant-based foods.

Beyond our own health, vegan eating is kind to the environment, too, with plant-based farming producing far fewer greenhouse gases than those farms raising livestock.

The Balanced Plate

The recipes in this book included a range of fruits, vegetables, legumes, grains, nuts, and seeds. This is in keeping with the principles of a balanced vegan diet, which provides all the macronutrients required by our bodies, including protein, carbohydrates, healthy (a.k.a. "good") fats, and fiber, plus other vitamins and minerals.

As a vegan it's important to be aware of the nutrients our bodies need and common food sources beyond dairy, seafood, and meat that provide them. The following information is drawn from the current US Departments of Agriculture and Health & Human Services *Dietary Guidelines for Americans*.

- **Carbohydrates:** Consume complex carbohydrates such as those found in brown rice, lentils, oatmeal, and quinoa rather than refined carbs found in processed foods such as cakes, cookies, and white bread.

- **Healthy fats:** Fats have long received a bad rap. However, "good" monounsaturated and polyunsaturated fats are an especially important part of healthy body function and can help reduce heart disease. We can get these from avocadoes, chia seeds, coconut and coconut oil, olive oil, and nuts.

- **Omega-3 fatty acids:** Omega-3s are very important for brain function and they lessen the risk of heart disease. The most common source of omega-3 fatty acids is fish, so it's important for vegans to include plant-based sources in their diet, which include Brussels sprouts, chia seeds, flaxseed, hemp seed, and walnuts.

- **Protein:** A common concern for vegan diets is a lack of protein. With some planning, though, it's easy to eat sufficient amounts, as it is common in many plant-based foods, such as legumes, nuts, seeds, whole grains, and some vegetables like broccoli, Brussels sprouts, and corn.

- **Vitamins:** Vitamins such as B_{12} and D are also important in our daily diet. These come from nutritional yeast and almonds, to name two sources.

Nearly all fruits, vegetables, legumes, nuts, and seeds have some amount of protein in them. The following ingredients are some of the most protein-rich foods to include in your diet.

BEANS: Full of protein, beans are incredibly versatile and come in many healthy varieties, including black beans, kidney beans, and pinto beans.

CHICKPEAS: Also known as garbanzo beans, these legumes are delicious when roasted and make a wholesome entrée when blended with spices.

LENTILS: There is a variety of lentils available, each of which has its own flavor and texture.

QUINOA: A superfood in a vegan diet, quinoa provides a great combination of protein and carbohydrates along with other nutrition. Enjoy quinoa in a pilaf or salad or as a breakfast bowl base.

TEMPEH: Made from cooked and fermented soybeans, tempeh has a heartier flavor and firmer texture than tofu.

TOFU: Also made from soybeans—and a good source of amino acids—tofu does not have a strong taste of its own, but absorbs the flavors used when cooking it.

Stocking up

Cooking becomes much easier when our kitchens are properly stocked with the right ingredients. Although there are no hard and fast rules on stocking up, keeping some basics in your kitchen can help healthy meals becomes enjoyable and easy. If you are new to the vegan diet, some staple foods will take you a long way in preparing delicious home-cooked meals without a lot of fuss.

You don't have to spend extravagantly on ingredients or spend hours roaming the health aisles to find what you need. The majority of ingredients in this book should be available in your local stores or nearest supermarket.

refrigerator

- Fruits, fresh and frozen
- Garlic
- Ginger
- Herbs, fresh
- Lemons
- Limes
- Maple syrup, pure
- Plant-based milk: almond milk, coconut milk, hemp milk, oat milk
- Sun-dried tomatoes
- Tempeh
- Tofu
- Vanilla extract
- Vegan butter
- Vegan cheeses
- Vegetables, including staples like onions, tomatoes, carrots, and greens

pantry

- Baking powder
- Beans, dried and canned
- Bread crumbs and panko
- Broth, vegetable
- Cocoa powder, unsweetened
- Coconut milk, canned

- Condiments: hot sauce, soy sauce, sriracha, vinegar
- Cooking spray, nonstick
- Flax meal
- Flour: all-purpose, chickpea, nut, whole-wheat
- Grains: brown rice, couscous, quinoa
- Legumes: chickpeas, lentils
- Nutritional yeast
- Nuts/nut butter
- Oil, olive
- Pasta
- Seeds: chia, flax, hemp
- Sugar, light brown

spice rack

- Black pepper, freshly ground
- Cardamom, ground
- Cayenne pepper
- Chili powder
- Cinnamon, ground and sticks
- Herbs, dried
- Nutmeg, ground
- Paprika
- Salt
- Turmeric, ground

Coconut milk is a useful and nutrient-packed ingredient to use in vegan cooking and baking in place of dairy. For the recipes in this book I use canned coconut milk, coconut milk packaged in a carton or Tetra Pak, and coconut cream, which comes in a can.

CANNED COCONUT MILK: Available in full-fat and lite varieties, coconut milk added to curries contributes a rich creaminess to the dish. Shake the can before opening it, to blend the "cream" that naturally separates from the more watery milk.

COCONUT CREAM: Thicker and creamier than coconut milk, this canned product comes in sweetened and unsweetened varieties.

COCONUT MILK IN A CARTON: This product is found mostly in the refrigerated section of the grocery store along with nut milks and is an alternative to dairy milk. It has a thinner consistency and can be used as a substitute for whole dairy milk. This form of coconut milk is available both sweetened and unsweetened, so read the labels closely to ensure you get the one you want. Coconut milk in a carton also comes in shelf-stable Tetra Paks. Do not confuse this product with coconut water, which is simply the water from the coconut.

About the Recipes

A number of features are provided with each recipe to help you navigate this book with ease. Firstly, you'll see that the recipes include an icon indicating the vessel that's used for cooking. Sometimes, at the end of a recipe, I provide a tip with the option of using another kind of cooking vessel to offer some flexibility.

This book is designed for people who already follow a vegan diet as well as for those who are new to the vegan diet and trying to find the right path to navigate through it. To make it even more user-friendly, the following labels are included among the recipes.

- Gluten-Free
- Nut-Free
- Soy-Free
- Under 30 Minutes, meaning it can be prepped, cooked, and served in 30 minutes or less

Each recipe also includes nutritional calculations—including calories, total fat, protein, carbohydrates, sodium, and fiber—to help you plan your daily diet.

Cinnamon French
Toast Bake, *page 16*

Chapter 2

Breakfasts

Tahini Banana Bread Oatmeal

GLUTEN-FREE, SOY-FREE, UNDER 30 MINUTES

SERVES 4 · PREP TIME: 10 MINUTES · COOK TIME: 2 MINUTES

4 cups unsweetened almond milk
2 cups old-fashioned oats
2 large bananas, mashed
2 tablespoons pure maple syrup
1 tablespoon tahini
1 tablespoon chia seeds
1 teaspoon ground cinnamon
1 teaspoon vanilla extract
2 tablespoons chopped walnuts

The rich, sweet flavor of banana bread is infused throughout this delicious oatmeal, which offers a tasty pairing of almond milk, bananas, and walnuts. This dish is nicely rounded out by the tahini, which brings bonus antioxidant and anti-inflammatory properties to the meal. Any leftovers can be refrigerated for up to 1 week.

1. In a pressure cooker, stir together the almond milk, oats, bananas, maple syrup, tahini, chia seeds, cinnamon, and vanilla. Close the lid and seal the valve. Pressure cook at high pressure for 2 minutes.

2. Carefully release the pressure and open the lid. Stir the oatmeal well, scraping the bottom with a spatula. Top with the walnuts to serve.

Cooking Tip: You can also make this dish in a stockpot or Dutch oven. Combine all the ingredients (except the walnuts) and cook, covered, over medium heat until almost all the liquid is absorbed. Turn off the heat, stir, and let sit for a few minutes before topping with walnuts and serving.

PER SERVING: Calories: 333; Total fat: 11g; Sodium: 176mg; Carbohydrates: 53g; Fiber: 9g; Sugars: 16g; Protein: 9g

Moroccan Tofu Scramble

GLUTEN-FREE, NUT-FREE, UNDER 30 MINUTES

SERVES 4 · PREP TIME: 5 MINUTES · COOK TIME: 20 MINUTES

2 teaspoons olive oil
1 teaspoon crushed garlic
1 cup chopped onion
½ cup chopped tomato
¼ cup sliced black olives
2 teaspoons Moroccan seasoning
15 ounces extra-firm tofu, drained, pressed, and crumbled

The Moroccan seasoning in this recipe adds an aromatic twist to a tofu scramble. You can put it on your toast or, if you are cutting down on carbs, simply enjoy it as is. You don't have to press tofu for very long because the liquid (if any) will be absorbed while cooking.

1. In a skillet over medium heat, heat the olive oil. Add the garlic and sauté for 30 seconds. Add the onion and sauté for about 2 minutes until translucent.

2. Stir in the tomato and cook for 4 to 5 minutes until mushy and well cooked.

3. Add the olives and Moroccan seasoning and cook, stirring, for about 30 seconds.

4. Add the crumbled tofu and mix well, scraping the bottom of the skillet. Cook for 5 to 7 minutes, stirring frequently and scraping the tofu from the bottom of the skillet with a spatula so it doesn't stick, until the tofu dries up nicely.

Variation Tip: Add ¼ cup chopped green bell pepper with the onion and ½ cup chopped kale with the tomato. If you want a spicy kick, skip the Moroccan seasoning and use turmeric and chili powder instead.

PER SERVING: Calories: 157; Total fat: 9g; Sodium: 35mg; Carbohydrates: 10g; Fiber: 3g; Sugars: 2g; Protein: 12g

Sheet Pan Buttermilk Pancakes

GLUTEN-FREE, SOY-FREE

SERVES 4 · PREP TIME: 20 MINUTES · COOK TIME: 20 MINUTES

Nonstick cooking spray

2 cups unsweetened
almond milk

2 tablespoons distilled
white vinegar, or freshly
squeezed lemon juice

1½ cups chickpea flour

½ cup almond flour

¼ cup chia seeds

¼ cup packed light
brown sugar

2 teaspoons baking powder

½ teaspoon salt

½ cup fresh fruit, such as
sliced strawberries or
blueberries

Pure maple syrup,
for serving

Whenever I feel nostalgic for traditional buttermilk pancakes, I quickly whip up this vegan substitute to satisfy my craving. Lower in fat than regular pancakes, these are also packed with superfoods in the form of chia seeds, chickpea flour, and almond flour.

1. Preheat the oven to 350°F. Coat a 9-by-13-inch sheet pan with cooking spray. Set aside.

2. In a large bowl, combine the almond milk and vinegar. Let sit for 15 minutes.

3. Add the chickpea flour, almond flour, chia seeds, brown sugar, baking powder, and salt. Whisk for 3 to 5 minutes until there are almost no lumps remaining. Pour the batter onto the prepared sheet pan.

4. Bake for 20 minutes, or until the top is set and dry. A fork inserted into the center of the pancake should come out clean.

5. Let the pancake cool on a wire rack for 2 minutes and cut it into four slices. Top with fruit and maple syrup to serve.

....

Cooking Tip: To make the pancakes on the stovetop, pour ¼ cup of batter onto a greased skillet over medium heat. Cook for 1 to 2 minutes until the top starts to dry. Using a spatula, flip the pancake and let it cook for 1 to 2 minutes more until it's lightly golden in color.

....

PER SERVING: Calories: 379; Total fat: 14g; Sodium: 633mg; Carbohydrates: 56g; Fiber: 15g; Sugars: 19g; Protein: 16g

Chocolate Chip Cookie Granola

GLUTEN-FREE, NUT-FREE, SOY-FREE, UNDER 30 MINUTES

SERVES 6 · PREP TIME: 5 MINUTES · COOK TIME: 20 MINUTES

1 cup old-fashioned oats
¼ cup vegan chocolate chips
¼ cup pure maple syrup
1 teaspoon extra-virgin olive oil
1 teaspoon vanilla extract
¼ teaspoon salt

This recipe provides a deliciously simple treat on a busy morning. Although the sweet flavors bring a decadent quality, the ingredients are more wholesome than those hidden in many regular granola bars.

1. Preheat the oven to 350°F.

2. On a 9-by-13-inch sheet pan, stir together the oats, chocolate chips, maple syrup, olive oil, vanilla, and salt. Spread the mixture evenly over the sheet pan.

3. Bake for 10 minutes. Using a spatula, stir the granola, spreading it evenly again. Bake for 10 minutes more until golden.

4. Let the granola cool on a wire rack for 2 minutes so it takes on a crispier texture.

Variation Tip: For a softer, more buttery finish, line a sheet pan with parchment paper. Combine all the ingredients in a large bowl, then stir in 1 tablespoon vegan butter, melted. Spoon the granola onto the prepared pan and spread it evenly with a spatula. Bake as instructed. Note that most vegan butters contain soy.

PER SERVING: Calories: 140; Total fat: 4g; Sodium: 98mg; Carbohydrates: 25g; Fiber: 2g; Sugars: 14g; Protein: 2g

Mixed Berry Grits

GLUTEN-FREE, UNDER 30 MINUTES

SERVES 4 · PREP TIME: 5 MINUTES · COOK TIME: 15 MINUTES

1 tablespoon vegan butter

1 cup sliced fresh
    strawberries

½ cup fresh blueberries

¼ cup fresh raspberries

2 tablespoons pure maple
    syrup, plus more
    as needed

1 tablespoon chia seeds

1 tablespoon hemp seeds

3 cups unsweetened
    vanilla almond milk

1 cup polenta grits

⅛ teaspoon salt

This warm bowl of grits is an easy breakfast complemented by the flavors of fresh mixed berries and vegan butter. Made from boiled cornmeal, grits are a Southern breakfast staple or side dish that is versatile enough to be enjoyed in a sweet or savory form.

1. In a stockpot over high heat, melt the butter, about 30 seconds.

2. Turn the heat to low. Add the strawberries, blueberries, and raspberries and stir until the berries are well coated with the butter.

3. Stir in the maple syrup, chia seeds, and hemp seeds to combine.

4. Stir in the almond milk. Increase the heat to high. Cover the pot and cook for 2 to 3 minutes until the mixture starts to boil.

5. Stir in the grits and salt. Adjust the heat to medium, re-cover the pot, and cook for 5 minutes. Open the lid and stir once. Turn off the heat, re-cover the pot, and let the grits sit for 1 to 2 minutes until the liquid is absorbed.

6. Taste and add more maple syrup, as needed.

Variation Tip: Instead of fresh berries, add 1½ cups sliced apple and ½ teaspoon ground cinnamon to the melted butter and cook as directed.

PER SERVING: Calories: 274; Total fat: 7g; Sodium: 199mg; Carbohydrates: 46g; Fiber: 5g; Sugars: 11g; Protein: 6g

Peanut Butter Quinoa Breakfast Bowl

GLUTEN-FREE, SOY-FREE, UNDER 30 MINUTES

SERVES 6 • PREP TIME: 5 MINUTES • COOK TIME: 12 MINUTES

2¾ cups unsweetened almond milk

1¼ cups quinoa, rinsed

¼ cup peanut butter

¼ cup pure maple syrup, plus more for drizzling

Pinch salt

Slivered almonds, for garnish

Fresh blueberries, for garnish

The combination of peanut butter and nutritious quinoa when cooked into a warm cereal is surprisingly delicious. Pair it with almond milk and nuts and you have a complete, wholesome breakfast. I like to bring extra sweetness to the bowl by adding fresh berries and drizzling a touch more maple syrup on top.

1. In an electric pressure cooker, stir together the almond milk, quinoa, peanut butter, maple syrup, and salt. Close the lid and seal the valve. Pressure cook at high pressure for 2 minutes.

2. Let the pressure release naturally for about 10 minutes. Quick release any remaining before carefully opening the lid.

3. Stir and serve warm with the almonds, blueberries, and more maple syrup.

Cooking Tip: You can make this in a stockpot. Combine all the ingredients in the pot over medium heat. Cover the pot and cook for 5 to 7 minutes, stirring every minute, until all the liquid is absorbed.

PER SERVING: Calories: 255; Total fat: 9g; Sodium: 155mg; Carbohydrates: 37g; Fiber: 4g; Sugars: 12g; Protein: 8g

Cinnamon French Toast Bake

SERVES 4 • PREP TIME: 10 MINUTES • COOK TIME: 40 MINUTES

2 tablespoons flax meal

Nonstick cooking spray

2 cups unsweetened almond milk

¼ cup pure maple syrup

2 teaspoons vegan butter, melted

1 teaspoon vanilla extract

¼ teaspoon ground cinnamon

4 cups (1-inch) whole-grain bread cubes

½ cup chopped walnuts

Vanilla powder, for seasoning

This French toast is a complete morning meal. The almond milk and vegan batter form a delicious treat that cooks to golden perfection. To up the nutritional content, I use whole-grain sandwich bread. For best results, use bread that is 2 to 4 days old so it absorbs more of the batter and holds its shape better while cooking.

1. In a small bowl, stir together the flax meal and 5 tablespoons water. Let sit for about 5 minutes.

2. Preheat the oven to 375°F. Coat a 9-by-13-inch sheet pan with cooking spray.

3. In a large bowl, whisk the almond milk, maple syrup, flax meal, butter, vanilla, and cinnamon, breaking up any clumps in the batter. Pour the mixture onto the prepared sheet pan.

4. Add the bread cubes and walnuts. Using a spatula, gently mix to combine, making sure to soak each bread cube in the mixture so no piece is left dry.

5. Bake for 30 to 40 minutes, or until the top is crispy. Season to taste with vanilla powder.

Variation Tip: Drizzle your favorite syrup over this French toast. Maple and blueberry are both good choices.

PER SERVING: Calories: 443; Total fat: 19g; Sodium: 467mg; Carbohydrates: 61g; Fiber: 12g; Sugars: 23g; Protein: 14g

Savory Vegetable Oatmeal

GLUTEN-FREE, NUT-FREE, SOY-FREE, UNDER 30 MINUTES

SERVES 4 · PREP TIME: 5 MINUTES · COOK TIME: 10 MINUTES

1 tablespoon olive oil

1 teaspoon fennel seeds

1 cup frozen mixed peas and carrots

½ cup chopped green bell pepper

2 cups old-fashioned oats

1 teaspoon salt

½ teaspoon chili powder

½ teaspoon ground cumin

¼ teaspoon ground turmeric

Why limit oatmeal to fruit and other sweet toppings when there are many savory flavor profiles that pair wonderfully with this ingredient? Here, whole-grain oatmeal cooked with Indian spices and vegetables combine for a hearty, healthy morning meal.

1. In a large stockpot over high heat, heat the olive oil. Add the fennel seeds and cook for about 30 seconds until aromatic.

2. Turn the heat to medium. Add the peas and carrots and sauté for 1 minute until they soften. Stir in the green bell pepper and sauté for 30 seconds more.

3. Add the oats, salt, chili powder, cumin, turmeric, and 4½ cups water. Stir to mix well. Adjust the heat to high and cook for 1 to 2 minutes until the oats come to a boil.

4. Turn the heat to medium. Cover the pot and cook for 3 to 4 minutes until the oats start to thicken.

5. Turn the heat to low, stir the mixture to avoid sticking, and cook for 1 minute more.

Cooking Tip: Any leftovers can be eaten like pilaf by pairing it with some raita. Simply warm the oats with ¼ to ½ cup water until they reach your desired consistency.

PER SERVING: Calories: 208; Total fat: 7g; Sodium: 613mg; Carbohydrates: 33g; Fiber: 6g; Sugars: 2g; Protein: 7g

Savory Mushroom Grits

GLUTEN-FREE, NUT-FREE, UNDER 30 MINUTES

SERVES 5 • PREP TIME: 5 MINUTES • COOK TIME: 15 MINUTES

1 tablespoon vegan butter

1 cup sliced white mushrooms

1 teaspoon dried oregano

1 tablespoon hemp seeds

½ teaspoon salt, plus more as needed

1 cup grits

This no-fuss recipe requires minimal prep: Simply toss everything into a stockpot. The mushrooms brown beautifully in the vegan butter. For an extra nutritional boost, I add hemp seeds, which are packed with protein and omega-3 and omega-6 fatty acids.

1. In a stockpot over medium heat, melt the butter. Add the mushrooms and sauté for 4 to 5 minutes until browned.

2. Turn the heat to medium-low. Add the oregano, hemp seeds, salt, and 3 cups water. Stir to combine.

3. Raise the heat to high. Cover the pot and cook for 2 to 3 minutes until the liquid begins to boil.

4. Turn the heat to medium-low and stir in the grits. Re-cover the pot and cook for about 5 minutes until all the liquid is absorbed. Turn off the heat and let the pot sit, covered, for 1 minute.

5. Stir. Taste and season with salt, as needed.

Variation Tip: Try rosemary or thyme instead of oregano.

PER SERVING: Calories: 151; Total fat: 4g; Sodium: 258mg; Carbohydrates: 26g; Fiber: 1g; Sugars: 1g; Protein: 4g

Savory Indian-Style French Toast

SOY-FREE, UNDER 30 MINUTES

SERVES 4 · PREP TIME: 5 MINUTES · COOK TIME: 10 MINUTES

1 tablespoon olive oil

1 teaspoon mustard seeds

½ cup chopped onion

¼ cup raw peanuts

1 cup chopped tomato

½ teaspoon chili powder

¼ teaspoon ground turmeric

8 bread slices, cut into 1-inch squares

1 teaspoon salt, plus more as needed

1 tablespoon ketchup

A savory twist on French toast, this dish is inspired by my mother's version of an Indian meal named *upma* that was a childhood favorite. Fragrant spices, peanuts, tomato, and onion are sautéed in a skillet with bread, lending a satisfying start to any day.

1. In a skillet over high heat, heat the olive oil. Add the mustard seeds and as soon as they begin to crackle, add the onion and peanuts. Sauté for 30 seconds.

2. Add the tomato and sauté for 2 to 3 minutes until mushy. Stir in the chili powder and turmeric.

3. Turn the heat to medium-low and add the bread, salt, and 1 tablespoon water. Mix well.

4. Turn the heat to low. Cover the skillet and cook for 3 to 4 minutes. Taste and season with salt, as needed. Stir in the ketchup.

Cooking Tip: If you wish to make the toast crispier, at the final step, let the mixture cook, uncovered, over high heat for 2 to 3 minutes, gently scraping the bottom of the skillet every minute so the bread doesn't stick.

PER SERVING: Calories: 331; Total fat: 12g; Sodium: 970mg; Carbohydrates: 52g; Fiber: 12g; Sugars: 11g; Protein: 15g

Spicy Shakshuka with Tofu

GLUTEN-FREE, NUT-FREE, UNDER 30 MINUTES

SERVES 8 · PREP TIME: 10 MINUTES · COOK TIME: 20 MINUTES

4 tablespoons olive oil

1 cup chopped onion

2 cups chopped tomato

2 tablespoons tomato paste

½ teaspoon sugar

2½ teaspoons paprika

2 teaspoons ground cumin

2 teaspoons salt

¾ teaspoon chili powder

1 (15-ounce) can cannellini beans, drained and rinsed

15 ounces extra-firm tofu, cut into 2-inch slices

Shakshuka is a Middle Eastern dish traditionally served with warm pita bread or challah. However, this tofu version is equally pleasing served on its own. If do wish to pair it with something and don't have any pita or challah handy, serve it on whole-grain toast.

1. In a skillet over high heat, heat the olive oil. Add the onion and sauté for about 2 minutes until it starts to brown.

2. Stir in the tomato, tomato paste, and sugar. Cook for 1 to 2 minutes until the tomato is mushy and well cooked.

3. Add the paprika, cumin, salt, chili powder, cannellini beans, and ¾ cup water. Turn the heat to medium and cook for about 1 minute until the mixture begins to boil.

4. With a spatula, spread the sauce into an even layer in the skillet and top it with the sliced tofu. Turn the heat to medium-low. Cover the skillet and cook for 10 minutes. Open the lid, flip the tofu pieces, and cook, covered, for another 5 minutes.

5. Turn off the heat and let sit for 2 minutes more, undisturbed, to allow any extra liquid to be absorbed.

. . . .

Variation Tip: If you like a really spicy breakfast, drizzle some sriracha over the top.

. . . .

PER SERVING: Calories: 360; Total fat: 20g; Sodium: 1,275mg; Carbohydrates: 31g; Fiber: 9g; Sugars: 6g; Protein: 19g

Tempeh Breakfast Casserole

NUT-FREE

SERVES 4 · PREP TIME: 10 MINUTES · COOK TIME: 30 MINUTES

1 tablespoon olive oil

3 cups broccoli florets

1 teaspoon dried oregano

1 (8-ounce) package
   tempeh, cut into
   ½-inch squares

¾ cup chopped red
   bell pepper

½ cup unsweetened
   coconut milk from
   a carton

1 teaspoon salt

1 teaspoon freshly ground
   black pepper

¼ cup vegan cream cheese

½ cup vegan panko

This easy casserole is a protein-packed breakfast topped with wonderfully crunchy vegan panko. The combination of the veggies, panko, and tempeh combine for a well-rounded nutritional profile.

1. Preheat the oven to 400°F.

2. In a Dutch oven over medium heat, heat the olive oil. Add the broccoli and oregano. Sauté for 2 minutes.

3. Add the tempeh and red bell pepper. Cook for 3 to 4 minutes.

4. Stir in the coconut milk, salt, and pepper. Cover the pot and cook for 3 minutes.

5. Turn the heat to low. Add the cream cheese and mix it well to blend with all the ingredients. Turn off the heat and top the mixture with the panko, spreading it evenly.

6. Bake for 20 minutes until golden-like in color.

Serving Suggestion: To convert this into a lunch or dinner meal, pair the dish with Persian Green Beans and Rice (page 59) or Herbed Brown Rice with Mushrooms (page 58).

PER SERVING: Calories: 275; Total fat: 14g; Sodium: 690mg; Carbohydrates: 24g; Fiber: 8g; Sugars: 3g; Protein: 13g

Harissa Black Beans and Sweet Potato Hash Browns

GLUTEN-FREE, NUT-FREE, SOY-FREE, UNDER 30 MINUTES

SERVES 6 · PREP TIME: 10 MINUTES · COOK TIME: 10 MINUTES

3 tablespoons olive oil

2 sweet potatoes, peeled and finely chopped

1 (15-ounce) can black beans, drained and rinsed

2 tablespoons chopped fresh chives

2 teaspoons ground harissa seasoning

1 teaspoon salt

1 teaspoon freshly ground black pepper

½ teaspoon paprika

1 tablespoon sriracha

This dish is a vegan variation of sweet potato hash browns turned into a complete meal with the addition of black beans. It features a delicious medley of spices—and some extra kick, courtesy of harissa powder.

1. In a skillet over high heat, heat the olive oil. Add the sweet potatoes and sauté for 4 to 5 minutes until they soften.

2. Stir in the black beans, chives, harissa, salt, pepper, and paprika. Turn the heat to medium. Cover the skillet and cook for 5 minutes until the sweet potatoes are cooked through and start crisping and forming a light golden layer on the pieces.

3. Stir in the sriracha.

Serving Suggestion: If you like a heartier breakfast, pair this dish with Moroccan Tofu Scramble (page 11) or the Spicy Shakshuka with Tofu (page 21) and serve on some toast.

PER SERVING: Calories: 176; Total fat: 7g; Sodium: 444mg; Carbohydrates: 23g; Fiber: 5g; Sugars: 3g; Protein: 5g

Breakfast Burrito Casserole

NUT-FREE

SERVES 6 · PREP TIME: 10 MINUTES · COOK TIME: 30 MINUTES

2 tablespoons olive oil

1 tablespoon minced garlic

1 cup chopped onion

1 cup chopped green
bell pepper

4 cups chopped tomato

2 (15-ounce) cans
black beans, drained
and rinsed

1 cup frozen corn

3 tablespoons taco
seasoning

2 teaspoons ground cumin

1 teaspoon salt

1 cup vegan mozzarella
cheese, divided

5 (6-inch) flour or corn
tortillas, quartered

This burrito casserole teams black beans and veggies sautéed in spices with a topping of tortillas and cheese. It makes a great weekend breakfast treat.

1. Preheat the oven to 350°F.

2. In a Dutch oven over low heat, heat the olive oil. Add the garlic and sauté for 30 seconds. Stir in the onion and sauté for about 2 minutes until golden brown.

3. Turn the heat to medium. Add the green bell pepper and sauté for 1 minute.

4. Add the tomato, cover the pot, and cook for 3 to 4 minutes until mushy.

5. Stir in the black beans, corn, taco seasoning, cumin, and salt, mixing until blended.

6. Add ½ cup water, stir, re-cover the pot, and cook for 2 minutes. Remove the lid and cook for 2 minutes more without disturbing the mixture.

7. Turn off the heat and sprinkle ½ cup of mozzarella on top. Add a layer of tortillas, making sure to cover the entire pan. Top with the remaining ½ cup of mozzarella.

8. Bake for 15 minutes, or until the cheese melts.

Serving Suggestion: Top the casserole with your favorite hot sauce to give this a stronger kick.

PER SERVING: Calories: 381; Total fat: 13g; Sodium: 1,063mg; Carbohydrates: 57g; Fiber: 11g; Sugars: 8g; Protein: 14g

Healthy Sheet Pan Frittata

GLUTEN-FREE, NUT-FREE, SOY-FREE

SERVES 4 • PREP TIME: 15 MINUTES • COOK TIME: 25 MINUTES

1½ cups chickpea flour

1 (15-ounce) can black beans, drained and rinsed

1 teaspoon salt

½ teaspoon cayenne pepper

¼ teaspoon ground turmeric

½ cup sliced red onion

½ cup sliced cherry tomatoes

Frittata is an Italian dish that is usually egg-based. In place of eggs, I use chickpea flour to bind it nicely and add protein. Although the chickpea flour won't rise like eggs, it lends a subtly nutty flavor and brings structure to the dish.

1. Preheat the oven to 350°F.

2. On a 9-by-13-inch sheet pan, using a spatula, stir together the chickpea flour and 1½ cups water until smooth.

3. Add the black beans, salt, cayenne, and turmeric and stir with the spatula, ensuring the batter is evenly spread in the sheet pan.

4. Gently place the red onion slices and cherry tomatoes over the batter.

5. Bake for 20 to 25 minutes, or until the frittata is cooked through and a toothpick inserted into the center comes out clean.

6. Let cool on a wire rack for at least 1 minute so the frittata will slide out of the pan easily. Cut the frittata into 4 pieces and serve.

Variation Tip: For added flavor, add green or red bell pepper slices along with the red onion and tomatoes and follow the recipe as instructed.

PER SERVING: Calories: 273; Total fat: 3g; Sodium: 591mg; Carbohydrates: 47g; Fiber: 13g; Sugars: 7g; Protein: 16g

Sweet Potato
Thai Soup, *page 30*

Chapter 3

Soups & Stews

Italian Wedding Soup

NUT-FREE

SERVES 6 · PREP TIME: 15 MINUTES · COOK TIME: 45 MINUTES

15 ounces extra-firm tofu

2 teaspoons Italian
seasoning

1 teaspoon salt

½ teaspoon
cayenne pepper

¾ cup panko

2 tablespoons olive oil

5 cups vegetable broth

1 cup fresh baby spinach

½ cup chopped carrot

½ cup couscous

Panko-coated tofu takes the place of meatballs in this vegan version of Italian wedding soup. I love to pair this with couscous for extra taste and texture. Ready in about 1 hour, it's a hearty and comforting bowl of goodness, especially during the colder months.

1. In a large bowl, crumble the tofu with your hands. Add the Italian seasoning, salt, and cayenne. Mix until well combined. Add the panko and mix until well combined. Shape the mixture into 12 small balls and set them aside.

2. In a Dutch oven over medium heat, heat the olive oil. Add the tofu balls in one layer. Cover the pot and cook for about 15 minutes until the bottoms of the tofu balls are brown. Gently flip the balls with a spatula or tongs, re-cover the pot, and cook for 10 minutes more.

3. Adjust the heat to high. Add the vegetable broth, spinach, and carrot. Cook for 5 minutes, stirring gently without breaking the tofu balls.

4. Add the couscous and cook for about 3 minutes more. Turn off the heat, re-cover the pot, and let rest for about 10 minutes until the couscous floats at the top of the soup.

Variation Tip: Instead of spinach, try another green—like kale or mustard greens.

PER SERVING: Calories: 219; Total fat: 8g; Sodium: 885mg; Carbohydrates: 27g; Fiber: 3g; Sugars: 3g; Protein: 11g

Black Bean Taco Soup

GLUTEN-FREE, NUT-FREE, SOY-FREE, UNDER 30 MINUTES

SERVES 6 • PREP TIME: 10 MINUTES • COOK TIME: 15 MINUTES

1 tablespoon olive oil

1 teaspoon minced garlic

½ cup chopped onion

1 (15-ounce) can black beans, drained and rinsed

½ cup frozen corn

2 tablespoons taco seasoning

5 cups vegetable broth

2 tablespoons chopped fresh cilantro

Salt

Made with simple pantry ingredients, this hearty and satisfying soup is a favorite go-to meal. I love to add lots of crushed tortilla chips to the soup and top it with avocado.

1. In a stockpot over high heat, heat the olive oil. Add the garlic and sauté for 30 seconds.

2. Turn the heat to medium. Add the onion and sauté for 3 to 4 minutes until golden.

3. Stir in the black beans, corn, and taco seasoning.

4. Add the vegetable broth and cilantro. Adjust the heat to high, cover the pot, and cook for 5 minutes. Taste and season with salt.

PER SERVING: Calories: 124; Total fat: 3g; Sodium: 594mg; Carbohydrates: 20g; Fiber: 5g; Sugars: 3g; Protein: 5g

Sweet Potato Thai Soup

GLUTEN-FREE, SOY-FREE, UNDER 30 MINUTES

SERVES 4 · PREP TIME: 10 MINUTES · COOK TIME: 15 MINUTES

4½ cups vegetable broth

3 sweet potatoes, peeled
and roughly chopped

¼ cup unsweetened
coconut flakes

2 teaspoons red
curry powder

1 teaspoon ground ginger

1 garlic clove, crushed

1 cup canned full-fat
coconut milk

2 tablespoons freshly
squeezed lemon juice

1½ teaspoons salt

¼ cup fresh cilantro

This rich and satisfying Thai-flavored soup uses simple ingredients and is quick and easy to make. No elaborate Thai curry paste is required here; an authentic taste is achieved with some red curry powder (readily available in spice aisles of supermarkets) along with ingredients like garlic, coconut milk, and lemon juice.

1. In an electric pressure cooker, stir together the vegetable broth, sweet potatoes, coconut flakes, red curry powder, ginger, and garlic. Close the lid and seal the valve. Pressure cook at high pressure for 10 minutes.

2. Carefully release the pressure and open the lid.

3. Using an immersion blender, blend the ingredients. Alternatively, transfer the soup to a standard blender, working in batches, if needed, and blend until smooth and creamy, 1 to 2 minutes. If using a standard blender, return the soup to the pot.

4. Stir in the coconut milk, lemon juice, and salt. Divide among 4 bowls, top with fresh cilantro and serve.

PER SERVING: Calories: 258; Total fat: 14g; Sodium: 1,500mg; Carbohydrates: 31g; Fiber: 5g; Sugars: 8g; Protein: 3g

Everyone's Favorite Minestrone Soup

NUT-FREE, SOY-FREE

SERVES 6 · PREP TIME: 10 MINUTES · COOK TIME: 25 MINUTES

2 tablespoons olive oil

1 tablespoon minced garlic

1 tablespoon chopped
    fresh basil

1 cup chopped onion

1 tablespoon tomato paste

1 cup frozen mixed
    vegetables (such as bell
    pepper, broccoli, onion,
    carrot, and corn)

6 cups vegetable broth

1 (15-ounce) can mixed
    beans, drained
    and rinsed

½ cup whole-grain
    fusilli pasta

1¼ teaspoons salt

1 teaspoon freshly ground
    black pepper

A hearty Italian classic made with vegetables, beans, and pasta, minestrone adapts wonderfully as a vegan dish. Pair it with some crusty bread and enjoy a delicious meal!

1. In a stockpot over medium heat, heat the olive oil. Add the garlic and basil. Sauté for 30 seconds. Add the onion and sauté for 3 to 4 minutes until golden.

2. Stir in the tomato paste and cook, stirring, for 30 seconds until the onion is well coated with the tomato paste. Add the mixed vegetables, cover the pot, and cook, stirring once or twice, for 1 minute.

3. Adjust the heat to high. Add the vegetable broth and mixed beans. Re-cover the pot and cook, stirring once or twice, for 3 to 4 minutes until the broth starts to boil. Lower the heat to maintain a simmer and cook for 5 minutes.

4. Raise the heat to high. Add the pasta, salt, and pepper. Cook, uncovered, for 5 to 7 minutes until the pasta is al dente.

Variation Tip: Minestrone was traditionally made to use up leftover produce, so feel free to add other vegetables or greens if you want an even heartier soup.

PER SERVING: Calories: 166; Total fat: 5g; Sodium: 1,052mg; Carbohydrates: 25g; Fiber: 6g; Sugars: 5g; Protein: 6g

Spicy Cabbage Roll Soup

GLUTEN-FREE, NUT-FREE, SOY-FREE

SERVES 6 · PREP TIME: 15 MINUTES · COOK TIME: 25 MINUTES

2 tablespoons olive oil

2 tablespoons finely chopped garlic

2¾ cups finely chopped baby bella mushrooms

2 tablespoons tomato paste

½ cup red lentils, rinsed

6 cups vegetable broth

5 cups chopped cabbage

1 teaspoon salt, plus more as needed

1 teaspoon freshly ground black pepper, plus more as needed

½ teaspoon cayenne pepper

2 tablespoons finely chopped fresh cilantro

All the satisfying flavors and ingredients of a cabbage roll can be found in this soup, minus all the preparation time. Just throw all the ingredients into your electric pressure cooker and enjoy this warm bowl of comfort.

1. On an electric pressure cooker, select sauté mode. Add the olive oil to warm. Add the garlic and sauté for 30 seconds. Add the mushrooms and sauté for 3 to 4 minutes until they release their juice and are well browned.

2. Stir in the tomato paste. Add the lentils and quickly stir to avoid burning.

3. Add the vegetable broth, cabbage, salt, black pepper, and cayenne. Using a spatula, stir until all the ingredients are well blended. Cancel sauté mode. Close the lid and seal the valve. Pressure cook at high pressure for 12 minutes.

4. Carefully release the pressure and open the lid. Stir in the cilantro. Taste and season with more salt and pepper, as needed.

Cooking Tip: This soup can be made in a stockpot or Dutch oven. Follow the same steps and cook over medium heat, stirring occasionally, for 35 minutes, or until the cabbage is soft and the lentils are nicely cooked.

PER SERVING: Calories: 124; Total fat: 5g; Sodium: 977mg; Carbohydrates: 17g; Fiber: 6g; Sugars: 6g; Protein: 6g

Lentil and Noodle Soup

GLUTEN-FREE, NUT-FREE

SERVES 4 · PREP TIME: 10 MINUTES · COOK TIME: 35 MINUTES

1 tablespoon vegan butter

1 teaspoon crushed garlic

1 bay leaf

½ cup chopped onion

5 cups vegetable stock

½ cup green lentils, rinsed

**1 cup rice noodles,
roughly broken**

**½ teaspoon salt, plus more
as needed**

**Red pepper flakes,
for garnish**

Whenever I find myself nostalgic for the flavors of chicken noodle soup, I turn to this equally tasty lentil substitute. It has a similarly comforting aroma and taste, and is just as soothing for a cold or sore throat.

1. In a stockpot over medium heat, melt the butter. Add the garlic and bay leaf. Sauté for 30 seconds. Add the onion and sauté for 1 or 2 minutes until translucent.

2. Add the vegetable stock and lentils. Cover the pot and cook, stirring occasionally, for about 25 minutes until the lentils are slightly more than half done but not soft yet.

3. Stir in the rice noodles and salt. Re-cover the pot and cook for 5 to 10 minutes more until the lentils are soft and the noodles are cooked.

4. Serve garnished with red pepper flakes.

PER SERVING: Calories: 307; Total fat: 4g; Sodium: 986mg; Carbohydrates: 58g; Fiber: 9g; Sugars: 4g; Protein: 9g

Tofu Ramen Bowl

NUT-FREE

SERVES 6 • PREP TIME: 10 MINUTES • COOK TIME: 25 MINUTES

3 tablespoons sesame oil

2 tablespoons red
miso paste

1 teaspoon dried
minced garlic

1 teaspoon garlic powder

15 ounces extra-firm tofu,
cut into ½-inch squares

5 cups vegetable stock

2 ramen cakes

1 teaspoon salt

Freshly ground black
pepper, or sriracha

2 tablespoons chopped
scallion

This super simple ramen soup is a Sunday night regular in my home. An incredibly healthy and protein-packed dish thanks to the tofu, its broth is enriched by the salty umami flavor of miso paste.

1. In a Dutch oven over high heat, heat the sesame oil. Turn the heat to medium. Add the miso paste, minced garlic, and garlic powder. Sauté for about 30 seconds until the miso paste loosens up.

2. Add the tofu, cover the pot, and cook for 10 minutes, gently stirring halfway through to keep the tofu from sticking, being careful not to break it up.

3. Add the vegetable stock, gently stir, and bring the soup to a boil. Cook for about 2 minutes.

4. Adjust the heat to high. Add the ramen cakes and salt and cook for 3 minutes. Using a fork, break up the noodles. Turn off the heat and let the soup rest, covered, for 1 to 2 minutes.

5. Taste and season with pepper and garnish the soup with scallion.

PER SERVING: Calories: 230; Total fat: 11g; Sodium: 1,090mg; Carbohydrates: 23g; Fiber: 3g; Sugars: 2g; Protein: 11g

"Hamburger" Soup

GLUTEN-FREE, NUT-FREE, UNDER 30 MINUTES

SERVES 4 · PREP TIME: 10 MINUTES · COOK TIME: 20 MINUTES

1 tablespoon olive oil

2 cups crumbled
   extra-firm tofu

1 tablespoon minced garlic

½ cup chopped tomato

1 tablespoon tomato paste

5 cups vegetable stock

½ cups chopped carrot

1 teaspoon celery salt

1 teaspoon freshly ground
   black pepper

1 teaspoon Italian
   seasoning

This soup has all the hearty savory goodness of a burger but uses only plant-based ingredients. It's a great dinner recipe if you're short on time—quickly sauté the base ingredients then let them pressure cook, and in about 30 minutes you're good to go!

1. On an electric pressure cooker, select sauté mode. Add the olive oil to warm. Add the tofu and garlic. Sauté for 4 to 5 minutes until the tofu starts to brown.

2. Add the tomato and tomato paste and mix well.

3. Stir in the vegetable stock, carrot, celery salt, pepper, and Italian seasoning. Close the lid and seal the valve. Pressure cook at high pressure for 10 minutes.

4. Carefully release the pressure and open the lid. Stir and serve.

....

PER SERVING: Calories: 189; Total fat: 10g; Sodium: 996mg; Carbohydrates: 13g; Fiber: 4g; Sugars: 4g; Protein: 14g

Herbed Tomato Bisque

GLUTEN-FREE

SERVES 6 · PREP TIME: 15 MINUTES · COOK TIME: 3 HOURS

4 cups vegetable broth

5 Roma tomatoes,
   roughly chopped

1 tablespoon vegan butter

1 teaspoon dried oregano

1 teaspoon dried parsley

1 teaspoon dried basil

1 cup canned full-fat
   coconut milk

2½ to 3 teaspoons salt

1 teaspoon freshly ground
   black pepper

¾ teaspoon sugar

Tomato bisque is a silky smooth version of classic tomato soup and is easily made with minimal fuss. A medley of herbs enriches the flavor, which pairs wonderfully with crusty bread. Making the soup in the slow cooker allows you to tend to other things for a few hours before putting the finishing touches on the soup.

1. In a slow cooker, combine the vegetable broth, tomatoes, butter, oregano, parsley, and basil.

2. Cover the cooker and cook on high heat for 3 hours.

3. Using an immersion blender, blend the soup until smooth. Alternatively, transfer the soup to a standard blender, working in batches, if needed, and blend until smooth. If using a standard blender, return the soup to the cooker.

4. Stir in the coconut milk, salt, pepper, and sugar. Let rest for 5 minutes before serving.

Cooking Tip: If you don't have a slow cooker, make this soup in a stockpot over medium-high heat on the stovetop. Reduce the cook time to 40 minutes.

PER SERVING: Calories: 131; Total fat: 10g; Sodium: 1,551mg; Carbohydrates: 10g; Fiber: 2g; Sugars: 7g; Protein: 1g

Quinoa Vegetable Chowder

GLUTEN-FREE, UNDER 30 MINUTES

SERVES 6 · PREP TIME: 10 MINUTES · COOK TIME: 20 MINUTES

2 tablespoons vegan butter

1 tablespoon minced garlic

1 tablespoon dried thyme

2 potatoes, peeled and chopped

1 cup chopped carrot

3½ cups vegetable broth

½ cup quinoa, rinsed

1 teaspoon salt

1 teaspoon freshly ground black pepper

½ cup canned lite coconut milk

Chowder is the ultimate comfort food, with a delicious blend of herbs and vegetables. The addition of protein-rich quinoa in this recipe makes a wholesome and complete meal. With minimal preparation or cooking involved, this dish is one of my favorites whenever I find myself short of time or inspiration in the kitchen.

1. On an electric pressure cooker, select sauté mode. Add the butter to melt. Add the garlic and thyme. Sauté for 30 seconds. Add the potatoes and carrot. Sauté for 1 minute.

2. Stir in the vegetable broth, quinoa, salt, and pepper. Close the lid and seal the valve. Pressure cook at high pressure for 5 minutes.

3. Let the pressure release naturally for about 10 minutes. Quick release any remaining pressure and carefully remove the lid.

4. Stir in the coconut milk.

Variation Tip: If you like your chowder extra creamy, before serving, stir in 2 tablespoons raw cashews and 3 tablespoons lite coconut milk.

PER SERVING: Calories: 175; Total fat: 6g; Sodium: 773mg; Carbohydrates: 27g; Fiber: 4g; Sugars: 4g; Protein: 4g

Easy Gumbo

NUT-FREE

SERVES 4 • PREP TIME: 15 MINUTES • COOK TIME: 1 HOUR

¼ cup vegan butter

2 tablespoons
   all-purpose flour

1 cup cauliflower florets

1 cup chopped okra

1 cup chopped tomato

½ cup chopped onion

4 cups vegetable stock

2 teaspoons Creole
   seasoning

½ teaspoon
   cayenne pepper

½ teaspoon salt

A popular stew hailing from Louisiana, gumbo is normally made with seafood and meat-based stock, but this easy vegan version achieves a similar Southern flavor profile with the help of vegetable stock, Creole seasoning, and cayenne pepper.

1. In a Dutch oven over high heat, melt the butter.

2. Turn the heat to medium-low. Add the flour and cook for about 30 minutes, stirring continuously, until it turns a caramel color. Be careful not to let the mixture burn.

3. Add the cauliflower, okra, tomato, and onion. Stir well to coat the vegetables completely with the roux. Cover the pot and cook for 4 to 5 minutes until the vegetables soften.

4. Adjust the heat to medium. Add the vegetable stock, Creole seasoning, cayenne, and salt. Stir to combine. Re-cover the pot and cook for 20 minutes before serving.

Variation Tip: Serve the gumbo over steamed rice for a more complete meal.

PER SERVING: Calories: 163; Total fat: 11g; Sodium: 956mg; Carbohydrates: 13g; Fiber: 4g; Sugars: 6g; Protein: 2g

Hearty Vegan Chili

GLUTEN-FREE, NUT-FREE, SOY-FREE

SERVES 6 • PREP TIME: 15 MINUTES • COOK TIME: 45 MINUTES

2 tablespoons olive oil

2 tablespoons minced garlic

2 bay leaves

1 tablespoon chopped celery

1 cup chopped onion

2 tablespoons tomato paste

1 cup chopped green bell pepper

1 (15-ounce) can black beans, rinsed and drained

1 (15-ounce) can kidney beans, rinsed and drained

½ cup green lentils, rinsed

2 teaspoons ground cumin

1 teaspoon paprika

½ teaspoon cayenne pepper

6 cups vegetable stock

1 teaspoon salt

Simmered in a richly seasoned broth, this bean and lentil chili is a protein-packed meal unto itself. If you don't have a Dutch oven, the recipe can just as easily be made in a stockpot following the same instructions.

1. In a Dutch oven over medium-high heat, heat the olive oil. Add the garlic, bay leaves, and celery. Sauté for 10 seconds. Add the onion and sauté for 1 to 2 minutes.

2. Stir in the tomato paste until well combined. Add the green bell pepper and sauté for 1 minute.

3. Stir in the black beans, kidney beans, lentils, cumin, paprika, and cayenne.

4. Turn the heat to medium. Stir in the vegetable stock and salt. Cover the pot and cook for 40 to 45 minutes until the lentils and beans are soft.

Variation Tip: This recipe pairs well with crushed tortilla chips and avocado slices. If I have any leftovers, I love to serve them over steamed rice for lunch the next day.

PER SERVING: Calories: 262; Total fat: 5g; Sodium: 966mg; Carbohydrates: 41g; Fiber: 13g; Sugars: 6g; Protein: 13g

Moroccan Lentil Stew

GLUTEN-FREE, NUT-FREE, SOY-FREE

SERVES 4 · PREP TIME: 10 MINUTES · COOK TIME: 3 HOURS

5 cups vegetable broth

1 (15-ounce) can chickpeas, drained and rinsed

1 cup red lentils, rinsed

½ cup chopped celery

¼ cup chopped scallion

1 tablespoon dried oregano

2 teaspoons Moroccan seasoning

1 teaspoon salt

1 teaspoon freshly ground black pepper

½ teaspoon cayenne pepper

This Moroccan-flavored stew couldn't be easier to make: Simply combine all the ingredients in a slow cooker and let it simmer. I use red lentils here, which cook more easily than other varieties and are famously high in protein.

1. In a slow cooker, combine the vegetable broth, chickpeas, lentils, celery, scallion, oregano, Moroccan seasoning, salt, black pepper, and cayenne.

2. Cover the cooker and cook on high heat for 3 hours until the lentils are completely soft. Stir before serving.

PER SERVING: Calories: 234; Total fat: 2g; Sodium: 1,259mg; Carbohydrates: 46g; Fiber: 16g; Sugars: 3g; Protein: 15g

Mushroom and Rice Stew

GLUTEN-FREE, NUT-FREE

SERVES 4 • PREP TIME: 10 MINUTES • COOK TIME: 40 MINUTES

2 tablespoons vegan butter

1 large rosemary sprig

2 cups sliced baby bella
   mushrooms

1 cup brown rice, rinsed

6 cups vegetable
   broth, divided

½ teaspoon salt, plus more
   for seasoning

Freshly ground
   black pepper

This simple and satisfying soup marries mushrooms, brown rice, and fresh rosemary. Whole-grain brown rice takes a little longer to cook than white rice, but is higher in nutrition. Even so, this recipe can be prepped, cooked, and served in less than 1 hour.

1. In a Dutch oven over high heat, melt the butter. Turn the heat to medium. Add the rosemary and cook for about 30 seconds until fragrant. Add the mushrooms and sauté for about 5 minutes until they begin to brown.

2. Stir in the brown rice and 5 cups of vegetable broth. Cover the pot and cook for 30 to 35 minutes until the rice is soft and chewy.

3. Reduce the heat to low. Stir in the remaining 1 cup of vegetable stock and the salt. Remove the rosemary sprig from the soup, pour the soup into bowls, and season with the pepper.

PER SERVING: Calories: 241; Total fat: 7g; Sodium: 1,147mg; Carbohydrates: 41g; Fiber: 4g; Sugars: 4g; Protein: 5g

African Peanut Stew

GLUTEN-FREE, SOY-FREE

SERVES 6 · PREP TIME: 15 MINUTES · COOK TIME: 3 HOURS, 40 MINUTES

5 cups vegetable stock

1 sweet potato, peeled and roughly chopped

½ cup creamy peanut butter

1 tablespoon tomato paste

1 teaspoon dried garlic

1 teaspoon ground ginger

1 teaspoon salt, plus more as needed

½ teaspoon cayenne pepper

1 cup fresh baby spinach

½ cup crushed raw peanuts

If you are a peanut butter fan, this stew is absolutely for you. The prominent flavor of peanut butter as the main ingredient along with crushed peanuts is extremely flavorful. The sweet potato helps thicken the soup and lend a sweetness. I usually add spinach for my kids, to include greens in their diet.

1. In a slow cooker, combine the vegetable stock, sweet potato, peanut butter, tomato paste, garlic, ginger, salt, and cayenne.

2. Cover the cooker and cook on high heat for 3 hours. Using a food masher, roughly mash the sweet potatoes in the slow cooker to thicken the stew a bit. Stir in the spinach and crushed peanuts. Re-cover the cooker and cook on high heat for 40 minutes more.

3. Alternatively, cook on low heat for 8 hours. Using a food masher, roughly mash the sweet potatoes in the slow cooker to thicken the stew a bit. Stir in the spinach and crushed peanuts. Increase the heat to high and cook for 30 minutes more.

4. Stir the soup. Taste and season with more salt, as needed.

PER SERVING: Calories: 238; Total fat: 17g; Sodium: 959mg; Carbohydrates: 16g; Fiber: 4g; Sugars: 6g; Protein: 9g

Fettuccine
Alfredo, *page 53*

Chapter 4

Rice & Grains

Easy Asparagus Risotto

GLUTEN-FREE, NUT-FREE

SERVES 4 • PREP TIME: 10 MINUTES • COOK TIME: 50 MINUTES

1 tablespoon olive oil

10 frozen asparagus
    spears, cut into
    1-inch pieces

½ cup chopped onion

1 cup arborio rice, rinsed

4 cups vegetable broth

1 teaspoon salt

1 teaspoon freshly ground
    black pepper

2 tablespoons vegan butter

1 tablespoon chopped
    fresh parsley

2 tablespoons grated
    vegan Parmesan cheese

This risotto brings all the flavor and comfort of the traditional Italian dish, minus the usual dairy products. The arborio rice is gently simmered in broth, with vegan butter and Parmesan bringing the signature creaminess.

1. In a stockpot over high heat, heat the olive oil. Add the asparagus in an even layer, cover the pot, and cook for 1 to 2 minutes until the asparagus softens and starts to brown. Turn the heat to medium. Using tongs, flip the asparagus. Cook for 30 seconds more.

2. Add the onion and sauté for 1 minute. Add the rice and sauté, stirring frequently so the rice does not stick to the bottom, for about 3 minutes.

3. Stir in the vegetable broth, salt, and pepper. Cook for 5 to 7 minutes until the broth starts to boil vigorously.

4. Turn the heat to medium-low and add the butter, stirring until it melts. Re-cover the pot and cook for 20 minutes.

5. Stir in the parsley. Re-cover the pot and cook for about 10 minutes more until all the liquid is absorbed.

6. Fluff the rice with a fork, cover the pot, and let rest for 2 minutes. Sprinkle with the parmesan.

PER SERVING: Calories: 285; Total fat: 9g; Sodium: 1,804mg; Carbohydrates: 44g; Fiber: 3g; Sugars: 4g; Protein: 6g

Turmeric Quinoa Pilaf

GLUTEN-FREE, SOY-FREE, UNDER 30 MINUTES

SERVES 6 · PREP TIME: 10 MINUTES · COOK TIME: 15 MINUTES

2 tablespoons olive oil

¼ cup raw cashews

1 cup chopped onion

1 teaspoon ground turmeric

½ teaspoon chili powder

2 cups quinoa, rinsed

Salt

1 tablespoon freshly squeezed lemon juice, plus more as needed

2 tablespoons chopped fresh cilantro

Although pilaf is commonly made with rice, this recipe uses naturally fluffy quinoa as a protein-rich substitute. Cashews add a touch of creaminess to the dish and turmeric brings a hint of spice and—bonus—anti-inflammatory properties.

1. On an electric pressure cooker, select sauté mode. Add the olive oil to heat. Add the cashews and sauté for 2 to 3 minutes until they start to turn golden.

2. Add the onion and sauté for 3 to 4 minutes until it starts to turn golden.

3. Stir in the turmeric and chili powder.

4. Add the quinoa and 4½ cups water. Season with salt and stir to combine. Close the lid and seal the valve. Pressure cook at high pressure for 3 minutes.

5. Carefully release the pressure and open the lid.

6. Using a fork, fluff the quinoa. Stir in the lemon juice, taste, and add more if desired. Garnish with cilantro.

....

PER SERVING: Calories: 312; Total fat: 11g; Sodium: 6mg; Carbohydrates: 46g; Fiber: 5g; Sugars: 6g; Protein: 9g

Paella

GLUTEN-FREE, NUT-FREE, SOY-FREE

SERVES 4 • PREP TIME: 10 MINUTES • COOK TIME: 40 MINUTES

3 cups vegetable broth

¼ teaspoon broken
saffron strands

1 cup arborio rice, rinsed

½ cup chopped onion

½ cup chopped red
bell pepper

1 teaspoon dried garlic

1 teaspoon dried thyme

1 teaspoon paprika

1 teaspoon salt

1 teaspoon freshly ground
black pepper

Although traditional paella is typically made in a special paella pan, this easy vegan version uses a Dutch oven instead. I highly recommend using saffron in this recipe for its floral notes and distinct flavor—and to achieve the signature bright color of the dish. You only need to buy a small amount, and any extra will store well for future recipes, such as Persian Green Beans and Rice (page 59) and Saffron Almond Fudge (page 132).

1. In a Dutch oven over high heat, cook the vegetable broth until hot but not boiling, about 1 minute. Turn the heat to medium. Add the saffron and cook, stirring, for 1 to 2 minutes until the broth turns a yellowish color.

2. Add the rice, onion, red bell pepper, garlic, thyme, paprika, salt, and pepper. Stir once. Adjust the heat to high and cook for 3 to 4 minutes until the liquid boils. Do not stir at this point or the rice will release starch.

3. Turn the heat to medium-low, cover the pot, and cook for 25 to 30 minutes until all the liquid is absorbed. If the liquid is not absorbed, turn off the heat and let the paella sit, covered, for about 3 minutes until all the liquid is absorbed. Do not stir or the rice will become creamy.

4. Open the lid, fluff the rice with a fork, and serve.

PER SERVING: Calories: 190; Total fat: <1g; Sodium: 981mg; Carbohydrates: 43g; Fiber: 3g; Sugars: 3g; Protein: 4g

Spicy Vegetable Rice Noodles

GLUTEN-FREE, NUT-FREE, SOY-FREE, UNDER 30 MINUTES

SERVES 4 • PREP TIME: 10 MINUTES • COOK TIME: 15 MINUTES

3 tablespoons sesame oil

5 dried red chiles, broken
    into pieces

1 tablespoon minced garlic

½ cup thinly sliced onion

2 cups frozen mixed
    stir-fry vegetables (such
    as peas, corn, carrots,
    broccoli, cauliflower, bell
    peppers)

1 teaspoon salt

1 teaspoon freshly ground
    black pepper

1 (6-ounce) package
    rice noodles

Packing a wonderfully spicy and garlicky punch, this super easy noodle dish is one of my all-time favorites. It's an aromatic and budget-friendly meal that calls for ingredients you likely have in your pantry—plus, it comes together very quickly.

1. In a stockpot over high heat, heat the sesame oil for 1 minute. Add the red chiles and garlic. Cook, stirring, for 30 seconds.

2. Reduce the heat to medium. Add the onion and sauté for 3 to 4 minutes until golden.

3. Add the stir-fry vegetables. Cook for about 2 minutes until they are soft.

4. Stir in the salt, pepper, and 1 cup water.

5. Add the rice noodles, breaking them as needed to fit in the pot. Turn the heat to low and pour 1½ cups water over the noodles. Rice noodles do not take long to cook but covering them well with water is important. Using tongs, toss the noodles. Cook, tossing continuously to soften the noodles, for 4 to 5 minutes until the liquid is absorbed. Let the noodles sit for 1 minute, then serve hot.

PER SERVING: Calories: 250; Total fat: 11g; Sodium: 592mg; Carbohydrates: 34g; Fiber: 2g; Sugars: 2g; Protein: 4g

Creamy Broccoli and Quinoa

GLUTEN-FREE

SERVES 6 · PREP TIME: 10 MINUTES · COOK TIME: 30 MINUTES

2 tablespoons vegan butter

¼ cup minced garlic

2 tablespoons almond flour

2½ cups canned
    unsweetened
    coconut milk

3 cups broccoli florets

1½ cups quinoa, rinsed

1 teaspoon salt

1 teaspoon red
    pepper flakes

½ cup unsweetened
    coconut cream

What I love most about this recipe is that it is casserole-like in its simplicity: Combine the ingredients in a Dutch oven, let them cook, and you're done. Broccoli florets and quinoa taste great with the creamy coconut sauce and results in a well-balanced meal.

1. In a Dutch over high heat, melt the butter. Add the garlic and sauté for 15 to 20 seconds until it turns brown.

2. Turn the heat to medium. Add the almond flour and sauté for 3 to 4 minutes until it becomes golden.

3. Stir in the coconut milk and 1 cup water. Cook, stirring continuously, for 3 to 4 minutes.

4. Turn the heat to medium-high. Add the broccoli, quinoa, salt, and red pepper flakes. Cook for about 10 minutes, stirring, until about half the liquid is absorbed.

5. Turn the heat to low. Stir in the coconut cream, cover the pot, and cook for about 10 minutes until all the liquid is absorbed.

PER SERVING: Calories: 460; Total fat: 29g; Sodium: 472mg; Carbohydrates: 38g; Fiber: 4g; Sugars: 5g; Protein: 9g

Couscous Tabbouleh

GLUTEN-FREE, NUT-FREE

SERVES 4 • PREP TIME: 10 MINUTES • COOK TIME: 25 MINUTES

⅔ **cup couscous**

½ **cup chopped fresh parsley**

1 teaspoon vegan butter

½ **teaspoon salt, plus more as needed**

1 teaspoon freshly ground black pepper, plus more as needed

1 cup chopped cucumber

½ **cup sliced cherry tomatoes**

¼ **cup sliced black olives**

2 teaspoons freshly squeezed lemon juice

This recipe has the flavors of Middle Eastern tabbouleh but uses couscous as its base instead of the traditional cracked wheat, resulting in a light and refreshing meal that's especially good in warm weather. The bright flavors of the lemon and parsley pair excellently with a medley of vegetables and the buttery couscous. Any leftovers can be eaten cold or at room temperature the next day.

1. In a stockpot over high heat, bring 3 cups water to a boil. Stir in the couscous, parsley, butter, salt, and pepper. Cook for 2 minutes.

2. Cover the pot, turn off the heat, and let rest for about 10 minutes until all the liquid is absorbed.

3. Using a fork, fluff the couscous and let cool to room temperature, about 5 minutes.

4. Stir in the cucumber, cherry tomatoes, olives, and lemon juice. Taste and season with more salt and pepper, as needed.

Serving Suggestion: This dish pairs well with pita bread or can be served with Skillet Mediterranean Chickpeas (page 82).

PER SERVING: Calories: 145; Total fat: 4g; Sodium: 435mg; Carbohydrates: 25g; Fiber: 2g; Sugars: 1g; Protein: 4g

Fettuccine Alfredo

UNDER 30 MINUTES

SERVES 4 · PREP TIME: 10 MINUTES · COOK TIME: 20 MINUTES

¼ cup vegan butter

2 tablespoons dried garlic

1 tablespoon
    dried oregano

½ cup nutritional yeast

5 cups unsweetened
    coconut milk from
    a carton

1 teaspoon salt

1 teaspoon freshly ground
    black pepper

1 pound fettuccine pasta

¼ cup fresh parsley

If you've ever found yourself nostalgic for the creamy, decadent flavors of fettucine Alfredo, this recipe is for you. This dairy-free version hits all the right notes with the help of vegan butter and coconut milk.

1. In a Dutch oven over medium heat, melt the butter. Add the garlic and oregano and sauté for 30 seconds. Add the nutritional yeast and sauté for 1 minute.

2. Turn the heat to high. Stir in the coconut milk, salt, and pepper and bring the mixture to boil. Cook for 1 to 2 minutes.

3. Turn the heat to medium. Add the fettuccine and cook, stirring occasionally to avoid sticking, for about 10 minutes until the pasta is tender but not mushy.

4. Turn off the heat, cover the pot, and let sit for 2 minutes. Stir, top with fresh parsley, and serve hot.

Variation Tip: In a high-speed blender, combine ¾ cup raw cashews, the nutritional yeast, garlic, oregano, and coconut milk. Blend until smooth and creamy. Set aside. Bring a stockpot or Dutch oven filled with water to a boil. Cook the fettuccine according to the package directions. Drain about half the water from the cooked pasta. Add the cashew sauce and stir to combine. Season with salt, pepper, and red pepper flakes and serve immediately.

PER SERVING: Calories: 635; Total fat: 19g; Sodium: 722mg; Carbohydrates: 95g; Fiber: 8g; Sugars: 5g; Protein: 21g

Cacio e Pepe

NUT-FREE, UNDER 30 MINUTES

SERVES 4 • PREP TIME: 10 MINUTES • COOK TIME: 15 MINUTES

1 pound spaghetti

1½ teaspoons salt

¼ cup vegan butter

¼ cup nutritional yeast

2 tablespoons freshly ground black pepper

2 tablespoons grated vegan Parmesan cheese

Vegan Parmesan takes the place of the customary Pecorino Romano in this dairy-free version of a Roman classic, whose name translates as "cheese and pepper." A cheesy texture is further achieved with the addition of nutritional yeast. Using the electric pressure cooker makes an already simple dish even more streamlined, with only one pot to clean when you're done.

1. In an electric pressure cooker, combine the spaghetti, salt, and 6 cups water. Close the lid and seal the valve. Pressure cook at high pressure for 4 minutes.

2. Carefully release the pressure and open the lid. Remove ½ cup of water from the pressure cooker.

3. Stir the butter, nutritional yeast, and pepper into the spaghetti. Cover the cooker and let rest for 1 minute. Garnish with the Parmesan and serve hot.

PER SERVING: Calories: 559; Total fat: 13g; Sodium: 1,042mg; Carbohydrates: 89g; Fiber: 6g; Sugars: 4g; Protein: 19g

Jambalaya

GLUTEN-FREE, NUT-FREE, SOY-FREE

SERVES 4 · PREP TIME: 15 MINUTES · COOK TIME: 1 HOUR

2 tablespoons olive oil

2 tablespoons
minced garlic

1 cup chopped onion

1 cup chopped tomato

1 tablespoon tomato paste

1 cup chopped green, red,
or yellow bell pepper

1 tablespoon
dried oregano

1 tablespoon dried thyme

½ teaspoon paprika

¼ teaspoon
cayenne pepper

1 (15-ounce) can
chickpeas, drained

1 (15-ounce) can red
kidney beans, drained

1½ tablespoons Creole
seasoning

3½ cups vegetable broth

1 cup long-grain white rice

1 teaspoon salt

1 teaspoon freshly ground
black pepper

A protein-rich combo of chickpeas and kidney beans stands in for shrimp and sausage in this plant-based version of jambalaya. With Creole seasoning and a tomato-based broth, it's just as enjoyable as the original, much-loved Southern classic.

1. In a Dutch oven over medium heat, heat the olive oil. Add the garlic and sauté for 30 seconds. Add the onion and cook for 2 to 3 minutes until translucent.

2. Add the chopped tomato and tomato paste and sauté for 3 to 4 minutes until the tomato is mushy.

3. Add the bell pepper and sauté for 1 minute. Stir in the oregano, thyme, paprika, and cayenne.

4. Add the chickpeas, kidney beans, and Creole seasoning. Cook for 3 to 4 minutes, stirring occasionally.

5. Add the vegetable broth, rice, salt, and black pepper. Stir to combine. Reduce the heat to medium-low. Cover the pot and cook for 45 to 50 minutes until all the liquid is absorbed. Fluff the rice with a fork and serve hot.

Cooking Tip: Texmati rice or basmati rice will lend the best texture and flavor to this dish, but you can use any long-grain white rice you have on hand.

PER SERVING: Calories: 504; Total fat: 9g; Sodium: 1,088mg; Carbohydrates: 90g; Fiber: 16g; Sugars: 7g; Protein: 17g

Vegan Herbed Brown Butter Cauliflower Rice

GLUTEN-FREE, NUT-FREE, UNDER 30 MINUTES

SERVES 4 · PREP TIME: 5 MINUTES · COOK TIME: 20 MINUTES

¼ cup vegan butter

1 (10-ounce) package frozen riced cauliflower

1 teaspoon dried garlic

1 teaspoon dried basil

1 teaspoon dried parsley

½ teaspoon ground ginger

¾ teaspoon salt

½ teaspoon red pepper flakes

If you're looking for a low-carb substitute for traditional rice, cauliflower rice is a nutritious and tasty alternative. Here, it's simply cooked with vegan butter and an aromatic medley of spices.

1. In a skillet over high heat, melt the butter. Cook, stirring frequently to keep it from burning, until the brown solids form, 3 to 4 minutes. Immediately remove from the heat.

2. Turn the heat to medium. Return the skillet to the stove and add the cauliflower, garlic, basil, parsley, ginger, salt, and red pepper flakes. Sauté for 10 to 15 minutes, stirring frequently, until the cauliflower is cooked through.

....

Serving Suggestion: This dish pairs well with the Creamy Mixed Vegetables (page 69) or Creamy Curried Lentils (page 80).

....

PER SERVING: Calories: 120; Total fat: 11g; Sodium: 572mg; Carbohydrates: 4g; Fiber: 2g; Sugars: 2g; Protein: 2g

Cilantro Rice with Black Beans

GLUTEN-FREE, NUT-FREE, SOY-FREE, UNDER 30 MINUTES

SERVES 4 • PREP TIME: 10 MINUTES • COOK TIME: 15 MINUTES

1 tablespoon olive oil

1 teaspoon minced garlic

1 cup chopped fresh
    cilantro

1 (15-ounce) can black
    beans, drained
    and rinsed

1 teaspoon ground cumin

½ teaspoon
    cayenne pepper

1 cup long-grain brown
    rice, rinsed

1 teaspoon salt

1 teaspoon freshly ground
    black pepper

I absolutely love the bright aroma and taste of fresh cilantro. The herb takes a starring role in this Mexican-inspired dish alongside black beans and brown rice. This recipe is great on its own, but you can top it with salsa, guacamole, and lemon juice if you want extra flavor.

1. In a stockpot over medium heat, heat the olive oil. Add the garlic and cilantro. Sauté for about 30 seconds until aromatic.

2. Stir in the black beans, cumin, and cayenne until well mixed. Cook for 1 minute. Stir in the rice, salt, black pepper, and 3 cups water. Increase the heat to high and cook until the mixture starts to boil.

3. Turn the heat to medium-low. Cover the pot and cook for 5 to 10 minutes until all the liquid is absorbed. Fluff the rice with a fork and serve.

Cooking Tip: If you have time, dry-roast some cumin seeds and grind them yourself to bring a smoky flavor and aroma to the dish. In a small nonstick skillet over medium heat, dry roast 1 tablespoon cumin seeds for 30 seconds to 1 minute until you get the strong smoky aroma. Immediately remove the skillet from the heat and let cool in the pan. Cumin seeds may turn dark in color, which is fine. Using either a clean spice grinder or mortar and pestle, grind the seeds. They do not need to be very fine in texture—a little chunky is totally acceptable.

PER SERVING: Calories: 307; Total fat: 5g; Sodium: 916mg; Carbohydrates: 55g; Fiber: 7g; Sugars: 1g; Protein: 11g

Herbed Brown Rice with Mushrooms

GLUTEN-FREE, NUT-FREE, SOY-FREE

SERVES 4 · PREP TIME: 10 MINUTES · COOK TIME: 45 MINUTES

3 tablespoons grapeseed oil

2 tablespoons chopped garlic

½ cup chopped fresh parsley

1 large rosemary sprig

¼ cup chopped fresh basil

2 cups sliced baby bella mushrooms

1⅛ cups extra-long-grain brown rice

1 teaspoon salt, plus more as needed

½ teaspoon red pepper flakes

There's something undeniably appetizing about fresh herbs cooked in oil. They give an extra flavor punch to a recipe, especially a rice dish. Here, fresh rosemary, parsley, and basil make a richly aromatic trio when combined with mushrooms and brown rice.

1. In a stockpot over medium heat, heat the grapeseed oil. Add the garlic, parsley, rosemary, and basil. Sauté for 30 seconds.

2. Add the mushrooms and cook, stirring occasionally, until browned, about 10 minutes.

3. Add the rice, salt, red pepper flakes, and 2½ cups water. Stir to combine. Turn the heat to high and cook for about 5 minutes to bring the rice to a boil.

4. Turn the heat to medium-low. Cover the pot and cook for 25 to 30 minutes until all the liquid is absorbed and the rice is tender.

5. Remove and discard the rosemary sprig. Fluff the rice with a fork. Taste and season with more salt, as needed.

PER SERVING: Calories: 300; Total fat: 12g; Sodium: 588mg; Carbohydrates: 43g; Fiber: 3g; Sugars: 1g; Protein: 6g

Persian Green Beans and Rice

GLUTEN-FREE, SOY-FREE

SERVES 4 • PREP TIME: 10 MINUTES • COOK TIME: 30 MINUTES

1 tablespoon grapeseed oil

1 cup thinly sliced onion

½ cup raw cashews

1 cup white basmati rice

2 cups frozen cut green beans

1 teaspoon salt

½ cinnamon stick

¼ teaspoon ground cardamom

¼ teaspoon broken saffron threads

This beautifully aromatic dish is great on its own and is a nice accompaniment to many Indian or Middle Eastern entrées. Saffron infuses a vibrant yellow color into the rice and enhances the flavors dramatically.

1. On an electric pressure cooker, select sauté mode. Add the grapeseed oil to heat. Add the onion and sauté for about 10 minutes until caramelized and golden brown.

2. Add the cashews. Sauté for about 2 minutes until they start to change color.

3. Add the rice and sauté for 2 to 3 minutes until aromatic.

4. Add the green beans and sauté for about 1 minute until soft.

5. Stir in the salt, cinnamon stick, cardamom, and saffron. Cancel sauté mode, close the lid, and seal the valve. Pressure cook at high pressure for 4 minutes.

6. Let the pressure release naturally for 2 minutes, then quick release any remaining pressure. Carefully remove the lid. Fluff the rice with a fork and serve.

Variation Tip: To make this dish more traditional, add ¼ cup raisins and ¼ cup dried cranberries in step 2.

PER SERVING: Calories: 314; Total fat: 11g; Sodium: 582mg; Carbohydrates: 46g; Fiber: 4g; Sugars: 2g; Protein: 7g

Mujadara Rice

GLUTEN-FREE, NUT-FREE, SOY-FREE

SERVES 4 · PREP TIME: 10 MINUTES · COOK TIME: 1 HOUR, 10 MINUTES

3 tablespoons olive oil

1 cup thinly sliced onion

1 bay leaf

1 cinnamon stick

1 tablespoon minced garlic

1 cup red lentils, rinsed

2 teaspoons ground cumin

1 cup long-grain brown
   rice, rinsed

1 teaspoon salt

Mujadara is a simple combination of lentils, onion, and rice that exists in various forms across the Middle East. This meal is great for the vegan diet, as the combination of lentils and rice makes a complete protein. Here, the lentils are cooked in mild spices and lightly seasoned, which will appeal to many palates.

1. In a Dutch oven over medium heat, heat the olive oil. Add the onion, bay leaf, and cinnamon stick. Sauté for 4 to 5 minutes until the onion is caramelized.

2. Add the garlic and sauté for 30 seconds. Adjust the heat to high.

3. Stir in the lentils and 5 cups water. Cook for about 2 minutes until the liquid starts to boil. Turn the heat to medium. Cover the pot and cook for about 10 minutes until the lentils are tender.

4. Adjust the heat to high again, add the rice and salt, and stir to combine. Cook for 3 to 4 minutes. Turn the heat to medium-low. Re-cover the pot and cook for about 35 minutes until the rice is tender and the liquid is absorbed.

5. Turn off the heat and let the rice rest, covered, for 10 minutes so it settles and absorbs any remaining liquid before serving.

PER SERVING: Calories: 378; Total fat: 13g; Sodium: 584mg; Carbohydrates: 60g; Fiber: 11g; Sugars: 1g; Protein: 14g

Garlic Fried Rice

NUT-FREE

SERVES 6 • PREP TIME: 10 MINUTES • COOK TIME: 25 MINUTES

2 tablespoons olive oil

¼ cup sliced garlic

2 cups extra-long-grain white rice

2 tablespoons low-sodium soy sauce

1 tablespoon distilled white vinegar

½ teaspoon salt

1 teaspoon freshly ground black pepper

1 tablespoon sliced scallion

Whenever I am short of ideas or ingredients, I simply toss together this wonderfully simple rice. It makes a light entrée or pairs very well with a variety of other recipes as a side dish, such as Chili Garlic Tofu and Peppers (page 66) or Sweet and Sour Tempeh (page 67).

1. In a stockpot over high heat, heat the olive oil. Add the garlic and sauté for 30 to 60 seconds until golden brown.

2. Add the rice, soy sauce, vinegar, salt, pepper, and 5 cups water. Stir to combine. Cook for about 2 minutes until the liquid begins to boil. Turn the heat to medium-low. Cover the pot and cook for about 20 minutes until the water is absorbed and the rice becomes tender.

3. Fluff the rice with a fork, sprinkle with the scallion, and serve hot.

Variation Tip: Add your favorite chopped vegetables to the stockpot along with the rice for a more substantial dish that can stand alone as a main course.

PER SERVING: Calories: 278; Total fat: 5g; Sodium: 499mg; Carbohydrates: 52g; Fiber: 1g; Sugars: <1g; Protein: 5g

Vegetable Couscous with Chickpeas

GLUTEN-FREE, NUT-FREE, SOY-FREE

SERVES 4 · PREP TIME: 10 MINUTES · COOK TIME: 25 MINUTES

1 tablespoon grapeseed oil
½ cup chopped onion
1 tablespoon chopped fresh basil
1 cup chopped green, red, or yellow bell pepper
½ cup frozen mixed peas and carrots
1 (15-ounce) can chickpeas, drained and rinsed
1 teaspoon salt
¼ teaspoon cayenne pepper
⅔ cup couscous

This idea is inspired from an Israeli recipe in which whole-grain couscous is combined with chickpeas. I add some vegetables to make it a more complete one-pot dish. It is perfect for hectic weeknights and makes for a great next-day lunch if you happen to have any leftovers.

1. In a Dutch oven over medium heat, heat the grapeseed oil. Add the onion and sauté for 2 minutes. Add the basil and sauté for 30 seconds. Add the bell pepper and peas and carrots, and sauté for about 1 minute. Stir in the chickpeas.

2. Add the salt, cayenne, and 3 cups water. Cover the pot and cook for 5 minutes.

3. Turn the heat to high. Remove the lid and cook for 2 minutes more.

4. Add the couscous. Cook, stirring, for about 1 minute, just until you see the liquid start to be absorbed. Turn off the heat, cover the pot, and let rest for 10 minutes. Fluff the couscous with a fork and serve hot.

Variation Tip: For a slightly different flavor profile, instead of cayenne pepper, add 1 teaspoon Moroccan seasoning and 1 teaspoon dried oregano and cook as instructed.

PER SERVING: Calories: 264; Total fat: 5g; Sodium: 597mg; Carbohydrates: 47g; Fiber: 8g; Sugars: 3g; Protein: 10g

Huevos Rancheros Rice

GLUTEN-FREE, NUT-FREE

SERVES 4 • PREP TIME: 10 MINUTES • COOK TIME: 50 MINUTES

1 tablespoon olive oil

½ cup chopped onion

2 cups chopped tomato

1 cup crumbled
   extra-firm tofu

2 tablespoons chopped
   jalapeño pepper

1 (15-ounce) can vegan
   refried beans

1 cup extra-long-grain
   brown rice, rinsed

1 teaspoon salt

1 teaspoon freshly ground
   black pepper

1 tablespoon freshly
   squeezed lemon juice

Huevos rancheros is a popular Mexican breakfast dish traditionally made with eggs and corn tortillas. Taking out the eggs and substituting rice for the tortillas makes this adaptation especially hearty. Make sure to read the ingredients labels when buying the refried beans because lard may be added in traditional preparations.

1. On an electric pressure cooker, select sauté mode. Add the olive oil to heat. Add the onion and sauté for about 2 minutes until translucent and aromatic. Add the tomato and sauté for about 2 minutes until mushy.

2. Add the tofu and jalapeño. Sauté for 4 to 5 minutes until the tofu starts to change color.

3. Add the refried beans and cook for 1 to 2 minutes, stirring, until the mixture loosens. Stir in the rice and cook for 2 minutes.

4. Stir in the salt, pepper, and 2½ cups water. Cancel sauté mode. Close the lid and seal the valve. Pressure cook at high pressure for 22 minutes.

5. Carefully release the pressure and open the lid. If the liquid has not been fully absorbed into the rice, select sauté mode again and cook for 4 to 5 minutes. Turn off the pressure cooker and let the rice rest until all the liquid is absorbed, 2 to 3 minutes more.

6. Stir in the lemon juice and serve hot.

PER SERVING: Calories: 385; Total fat: 10g; Sodium: 1,078mg; Carbohydrates: 58g; Fiber: 9g; Sugars: 3g; Protein: 17g

Skillet Mediterranean
Chickpeas, *page 82*

Chapter 5

Vegetable Mains

Chili Garlic Tofu and Peppers

NUT-FREE, UNDER 30 MINUTES

SERVES 4 • PREP TIME: 10 MINUTES • COOK TIME: 10 MINUTES

½ cup low-sodium
soy sauce

2 tablespoons distilled
white vinegar

1 teaspoon cornstarch

2 tablespoons sriracha

1 tablespoon pure
maple syrup

15 ounces extra-firm tofu,
drained, pressed, and
cut into 1-inch cubes

½ cup chopped green
bell pepper

1 tablespoon sliced
scallion

Freshly ground
black pepper

This Asian-inspired tofu and pepper recipe comes together in a skillet in just 20 minutes. This subtly sweet and sour dish has an appealingly vinegary tang.

1. Heat a skillet over high heat for about 30 seconds. Turn off the heat and immediately whisk in the soy sauce, vinegar, and cornstarch until smooth, 1 to 2 minutes.

2. Turn the heat to low. Add the sriracha and maple syrup to the cornstarch mixture. Whisk for 30 seconds.

3. Add the tofu and green bell pepper. Using a spatula, gently mix until the tofu is completely covered in the sauce. Cover the skillet and cook for 5 to 7 minutes until the tofu is cooked through.

4. Taste and season with pepper. Garnish with scallion.

....

Serving Suggestion: This recipe pairs well with the Spicy Vegetable Rice Noodles (page 49) or Garlic Fried Rice (page 61).

....

PER SERVING: Calories: 149; Total fat: 5g; Sodium: 1,332mg; Carbohydrates: 13g; Fiber: 2g; Sugars: 5g; Protein: 13g

Sweet and Sour Tempeh

NUT-FREE, UNDER 30 MINUTES

SERVES 4 • PREP TIME: 10 MINUTES • COOK TIME: 20 MINUTES

2 tablespoons olive oil

8 ounces tempeh, cut into
   1-inch squares

1 tablespoon cornstarch

½ cup low-sodium
   soy sauce

¼ cup distilled
   white vinegar

2 tablespoons pure
   maple syrup

2 tablespoons ketchup

½ cup (1-inch) cubed onion

½ cup (1-inch) cubed red
   bell pepper

Freshly ground
   black pepper

Here is a healthy twist on a Chinese takeout favorite. My daughter loves the sweet and sour sauce, so I often make this dish for her and her friends when we have playdates. For the grown-ups, I like to sprinkle red pepper flakes on top to spice it up a bit.

1. In a skillet over medium heat, heat the olive oil.

2. Turn the heat to low. Add the tempeh and cornstarch and gently mix with spatula until the tempeh is covered with cornstarch and oil and there are no lumps.

3. Adjust the heat to medium-high and cook for 4 to 5 minutes until the tempeh is brown. Using a spatula, flip the tempeh and cook for 3 to 4 minutes more.

4. Turn the heat to medium-low. Add the soy sauce, vinegar, maple syrup, and ketchup and gently stir to combine.

5. Raise the heat to medium. Gently stir in the onion and red bell pepper. Cover the skillet and cook for 5 minutes. Taste and season with pepper.

Serving Suggestion: Serve this with the Garlic Fried Rice (page 61) or with Vegan Herbed Brown Butter Cauliflower Rice (page 56).

PER SERVING: Calories: 253; Total fat: 13g; Sodium: 1,884mg; Carbohydrates: 24g; Fiber: 6g; Sugars: 8g; Protein: 12g

Chickpea Tikka Masala

GLUTEN-FREE, SOY-FREE, UNDER 30 MINUTES

SERVES 4 • PREP TIME: 10 MINUTES • COOK TIME: 20 MINUTES

1 tablespoon olive oil

1 tablespoon
crushed garlic

1 tablespoon crushed
peeled fresh ginger

½ cup chopped onion

2 tablespoons
tomato paste

1 tablespoon
garam masala

½ teaspoon ground
turmeric

1 (15-ounce) can
chickpeas, drained
and rinsed

1½ cups unsweetened
coconut milk from
a carton

1 teaspoon salt

¼ teaspoon sugar

This vegan version of an Indian classic swaps chicken for chickpeas, a lovely source of protein that holds up well when cooked with flavorful spices. A secret weapon here is the use of garam masala, a fragrant blend of pepper, cloves, nutmeg, cardamom, and cumin that's commonly available in grocery stores. With a sauce thickened by coconut milk, this dish is easy to cook and delightful to devour.

1. In a stockpot over medium heat, heat the olive oil. Add the garlic and ginger and sauté for 30 seconds until they start to brown. Turn the heat to medium-low. Add the onion and sauté for 5 minutes until brown.

2. Stir in the tomato paste until it loosens up. Add the garam masala and turmeric. Cook, stirring, for 1 to 2 minutes until aromatic.

3. Stir in the chickpeas, stirring until they are covered with the tomato paste mixture.

4. Turn the heat to medium-high and add the coconut milk, salt, and sugar. Cook, stirring occasionally, for 5 minutes. Reduce the heat to medium-low and cook for 5 minutes more.

Serving Suggestion: Pour the masala over steamed rice, Persian Green Beans and Rice (page 59), or serve with naan.

PER SERVING: Calories: 177; Total fat: 6g; Sodium: 654mg; Carbohydrates: 25g; Fiber: 7g; Sugars: 3g; Protein: 6g

Creamy Mixed Vegetables

GLUTEN-FREE

SERVES 6 · PREP TIME: 10 MINUTES · COOK TIME: 40 MINUTES

1 tablespoon vegan butter

1 tablespoon minced garlic

2 teaspoons crushed peeled fresh ginger

½ cup chopped onion

1 cup chopped tomato

2 cups frozen mixed vegetables (such as peas, carrots, corn, broccoli, green beans, and bell peppers)

3 cups unsweetened coconut milk from a carton

2 teaspoons cornstarch

1 teaspoon salt

½ teaspoon cayenne pepper

2 tablespoons unsweetened coconut cream

With the vegetables in this dish sautéed in a lightly creamy and richly flavored sauce, your family won't even realize they are eating a healthy meal. And using frozen vegetables cuts down on prep time and still offers their full nutritional value.

1. In a stockpot over medium-high heat, melt the butter. Add the garlic and ginger and sauté for about 30 seconds until brown. Add the onion and sauté for 3 to 4 minutes until brown.

2. Add the tomato, cover the pot, and cook for 3 to 4 minutes until the tomato is mushy and releases its juice.

3. Stir in the mixed vegetables.

4. Stir in the coconut milk and cornstarch. Sauté for about 1 minute until there are no lumps. Add the salt and cayenne, re-cover the pot, and cook, stirring occasionally, for 25 to 30 minutes until the sauce thickens and the vegetables are cooked through.

5. Stir in the coconut cream and serve.

Serving Suggestion: Spoon over Persian Green Beans and Rice (page 59) or steamed rice.

PER SERVING: Calories: 89; Total fat: 5g; Sodium: 438mg; Carbohydrates: 10g; Fiber: 2g; Sugars: 4g; Protein: 1g

Broccoli Tempeh Casserole

GLUTEN-FREE

SERVES 4 · PREP TIME: 10 MINUTES · COOK TIME: 30 MINUTES

1 tablespoon vegan butter

1 teaspoon dried garlic

1 teaspoon dried oregano

¼ cup almond flour

2 cups unsweetened
   coconut milk from
   a carton

1 teaspoon salt

1 teaspoon freshly ground
   black pepper

1 cup shredded vegan
   mozzarella cheese

2 cups broccoli florets

8 ounces tempeh, cut into
   ½-inch squares

I love to make this casserole on rainy days when I'm craving something warm and comforting. The broccoli and tempeh are hearty and delicious in a delectably creamy sauce.

1. In a Dutch oven over medium heat, melt the butter. Add the garlic and oregano and sauté for about 30 seconds until aromatic.

2. Add the almond flour and sauté for about 2 minutes until the mixture starts to turn brown.

3. Add the coconut milk, salt, and pepper. Cook, stirring occasionally, for about 2 minutes until the mixture is very warm but not boiling.

4. Stir in the mozzarella cheese and cook for 1 minute more.

5. Add the broccoli and tempeh and stir. Turn the heat to high, cover the pot, and bring the mixture to a boil, 1 to 2 minutes. Stir the mixture well, scraping the bottom of the Dutch oven. Turn the heat to medium-low and cook for 5 minutes more.

6. Turn the heat to medium and cook for 10 minutes more, stirring occasionally, until the sauce is smooth and creamy. Remove from the heat, cover, and let rest for 5 minutes before serving.

PER SERVING: Calories: 307; Total fat: 22g; Sodium: 729mg; Carbohydrates: 16g; Fiber: 8g; Sugars: 2g; Protein: 13g

Green Bean Casserole

NUT-FREE

SERVES 6 · PREP TIME: 10 MINUTES · COOK TIME: 30 MINUTES

2 tablespoons vegan butter

1 tablespoon dried garlic

1 tablespoon
all-purpose flour

2 cups vegetable broth

½ cup unsweetened
coconut milk from
a carton

1 teaspoon salt

1 teaspoon freshly ground
black pepper

1 (12-ounce) package
frozen green beans

1½ cups
French-fried onions

This is the green bean casserole to serve at holiday celebrations like Thanksgiving. The green beans are sautéed to tender perfection and complemented by the crunchy texture of fried onions. Everyone will love this.

1. Preheat the oven to 400°F.

2. In a Dutch oven over high heat, melt the butter. Add the garlic and flour and sauté for 3 to 4 minutes until the mixture starts to turn golden.

3. Turn the heat to medium. Add the vegetable broth and coconut milk and bring to a boil, stirring continuously, about 2 minutes. Add the salt and pepper and stir to combine.

4. Add the green beans, cover the pot, and cook for 3 to 4 minutes until the beans are crisp-tender.

5. Place the Dutch oven in the oven and bake for 15 minutes.

6. Sprinkle the fried onions over the beans and let rest for 2 minutes.

Variation Tip: Add 1 cup sliced mushrooms when you add the green beans for a heartier, earthier version of this favorite side dish.

PER SERVING: Calories: 151; Total fat: 11g; Sodium: 726mg; Carbohydrates: 11g; Fiber: 1g; Sugars: 1g; Protein: 1g

Saucy Beans Skillet

GLUTEN-FREE, NUT-FREE, SOY-FREE

SERVES 4 · PREP TIME: 10 MINUTES · COOK TIME: 30 MINUTES

2 tablespoons olive oil
1 teaspoon dried oregano
1 teaspoon dried basil
1 teaspoon dried parsley
1 teaspoon dried garlic
2½ cups chopped tomato
2 tablespoons ketchup
**1 (15-ounce) can
   cannellini beans, rinsed
   and drained**
1 teaspoon salt

A hearty meal in its own right, this dish pairs cannellini beans with all the familiar herbs and spices of an Italian pasta sauce. Serve it with pasta if you wish, but I love this skillet dish on its own as a low-carb treat.

1. In a skillet over high heat, heat the olive oil. Add the oregano, basil, parsley, and garlic. Sauté for about 30 seconds until aromatic.

2. Stir in the tomato and ketchup. Turn the heat to medium, cover the skillet, and cook for 10 minutes. Using a spatula, crush the tomatoes.

3. Turn the heat to high. Add the cannellini beans, salt, and 2 cups water. Stir to combine. Re-cover the skillet and cook for 15 minutes. Stir and serve hot.

PER SERVING: Calories: 196; Total fat: 8g; Sodium: 672mg; Carbohydrates: 27g; Fiber: 6g; Sugars: 4g; Protein: 7g

Creamy Peas and Potatoes

GLUTEN-FREE, SOY-FREE, UNDER 30 MINUTES

SERVES 5 • PREP TIME: 10 MINUTES • COOK TIME: 15 MINUTES

2½ cups (½-inch) cubed Yukon Gold potatoes

3 cups unsweetened coconut milk from a carton

1 cup green peas

1 teaspoon salt

1 teaspoon freshly ground black pepper

1 teaspoon dried oregano

1 teaspoon dried basil

½ teaspoon red pepper flakes

2 tablespoons unsweetened coconut cream

It doesn't get much easier than this creamy pea and potato combo. A substantial meal when served over steamed rice or quinoa, it requires very little prep or supervision when made in an electric pressure cooker.

1. In an electric pressure cooker, stir together the potatoes, coconut milk, peas, salt, black pepper, oregano, basil, and red pepper flakes. Close the lid and seal the valve. Pressure cook at high pressure for 5 minutes.

2. Carefully release the pressure and open the lid. Stir in the coconut cream.

Cooking Tip: To make this on the stovetop, place the ingredients in a stockpot over medium-high heat, cover, and cook, stirring frequently, for 20 minutes, or until the potatoes are soft.

PER SERVING: Calories: 122; Total fat: 4g; Sodium: 512mg; Carbohydrates: 19g; Fiber: 5g; Sugars: 3g; Protein: 3g

Cauliflower au Gratin

NUT-FREE

SERVES 6 · PREP TIME: 10 MINUTES · COOK TIME: 45 MINUTES

2 tablespoons vegan butter

2 tablespoons
   minced garlic

2 tablespoons
   all-purpose flour

3 cups canned
   unsweetened
   coconut milk

¼ cup nutritional yeast

½ teaspoon salt

Freshly ground
   black pepper

5 cups cauliflower florets

2 cups shredded
   vegan mozzarella
   cheese, divided

½ cup bread crumbs,
   or panko

Traditional gratins tend to be loaded with calories due to a wealth of dairy, but this version lightens the classic French recipe with just-as-delicious results.

1. Preheat the oven to 350°F.

2. In a Dutch oven over medium-high heat, melt the butter. Add the garlic and sauté for 30 seconds until it begins to brown. Add the flour and sauté for about 2 minutes until golden brown.

3. Turn the heat to low and add the coconut milk. Turn the heat to high and stir until there are no lumps. Cook for 1 to 2 minutes until the mixture comes to a boil.

4. Add the nutritional yeast and salt and season with pepper. Cook for 2 to 3 minutes, stirring, until the mixture starts to thicken.

5. Add the cauliflower and cook for 10 to 15 minutes until tender.

6. Turn off the heat and sprinkle 1 cup of mozzarella cheese in an even layer over the top. Sprinkle the bread crumbs in an even layer over the mozzarella. Top with the remaining 1 cup of mozzarella.

7. Bake for 15 minutes, or until the cheese melts completely.

8. Cover the gratin with a lid and let stand for 5 minutes before serving.

PER SERVING: Calories: 427; Total fat: 36g; Sodium: 464mg; Carbohydrates: 20g; Fiber: 5g; Sugars: 3g; Protein: 8g

Eggplant with Miso Aioli

UNDER 30 MINUTES

SERVES 4 • PREP TIME: 10 MINUTES • COOK TIME: 20 MINUTES

2 tablespoons olive oil

2 medium eggplants, cut
   into 1-inch cubes

½ teaspoon salt

2 teaspoons freshly ground
   black pepper

1 teaspoon distilled
   white vinegar

⅓ cup unsweetened
   coconut milk from
   a carton

¼ cup miso paste

Cooked brown rice,
   for serving

Buy fresh, firm eggplants to achieve the right texture in this simple dish. The delicious miso and coconut milk aioli is irresistible.

1. In a skillet over medium-high heat, heat the olive oil. Add the eggplant, cover the skillet, and cook for 5 minutes.

2. Turn the heat to medium. Add the salt, pepper, and vinegar and stir to combine. Turn the heat to medium-low, re-cover the skillet, and cook for about 10 minutes until the eggplant is tender but not mushy.

3. Using a spatula, stir again, gently scraping the bottom of the skillet. Add the coconut milk and miso paste and continue to stir gently until the miso paste loosens and dissolves in the milk, making sure not to crush the eggplant.

4. Raise the heat to medium, re-cover the skillet, and cook for 2 minutes. Stir gently to combine and serve over brown rice.

Serving Suggestion: Try this over Garlic Fried Rice (page 61) for a little extra flavor.

PER SERVING: Calories: 143; Total fat: 8g; Sodium: 340mg; Carbohydrates: 18g; Fiber: 7g; Sugars: 11g; Protein: 3g

Ratatouille

GLUTEN-FREE, NUT-FREE, SOY-FREE

SERVES 4 • PREP TIME: 10 MINUTES • COOK TIME: 25 MINUTES

1 tablespoon olive oil

1 bay leaf

1 tablespoon minced garlic

1 cup chopped onion

2½ cups chopped tomato

2 teaspoons dried oregano

4 cups (½-inch) cubed eggplant

2 cups (½-inch) cubed zucchini

1 teaspoon salt

1 teaspoon freshly ground black pepper

Originating from Nice, in France, ratatouille is a simple tomato-based stew that usually includes eggplant and zucchini. Although you may prefer to serve it warm, ratatouille is traditionally eaten at room temperature or even cold.

1. In a skillet over high heat, heat the olive oil. Add the bay leaf and garlic and sauté for about 30 seconds until the garlic starts to brown. Add the onion and sauté for 2 to 3 minutes until golden.

2. Stir in tomato and oregano. Cover the skillet and cook for 3 to 4 minutes until the tomato is mushy.

3. Turn the heat to medium. Add the eggplant, zucchini, salt, and pepper. Stir to combine. Re-cover the skillet and cook for 15 minutes. Stir again and serve at the temperature you desire.

Serving Suggestion: Cut a French baguette into slices, toast them, and serve on the side.

PER SERVING: Calories: 111; Total fat: 4g; Sodium: 599mg; Carbohydrates: 19g; Fiber: 6g; Sugars: 9g; Protein: 3g

Chimichurri Lentil Curry

GLUTEN-FREE, NUT-FREE, SOY-FREE, UNDER 30 MINUTES

SERVES 4 · PREP TIME: 10 MINUTES · COOK TIME: 15 MINUTES

1 tablespoon olive oil

1 cup chopped
   fresh parsley

½ cup chopped fresh
   cilantro

1½ teaspoons
   minced garlic

1 cup green lentils, rinsed

2 teaspoons freshly
   squeezed lemon juice

1 teaspoon salt

1 teaspoon freshly ground
   black pepper

Steamed rice or quinoa, for
   serving (optional)

An Argentinian favorite, chimichurri brings together ingredients like parsley, garlic, and oregano to form a zingy table condiment. In this recipe, I've infused its base ingredients with lentils to make a wholesome curry with a fresh, tangy flavor.

1. On an electric pressure cooker, select sauté mode. Add the olive oil to heat. Add the parsley and cilantro and sauté for about 2 minutes until aromatic. Add the garlic and sauté for 30 seconds. Add the lentils and cook, stirring, for 1 minute.

2. Stir in the lemon juice, salt, pepper, and 3 cups water. Cancel sauté mode. Close the lid and seal the valve. Pressure cook at high pressure for 5 minutes.

3. Carefully release the pressure, open the lid, and stir. Serve hot over steamed rice or quinoa (if using).

....

Cooking Tip: This recipe can be made on the stovetop in a stockpot or a Dutch oven. Heat the oil over medium heat and sauté the parsley and cilantro for 30 seconds. Add the garlic and lentils and sauté for 1 minute. Add the remaining ingredients, cover the pot, and cook for 15 to 20 minutes until the lentils are soft.

....

PER SERVING: Calories: 192; Total fat: 5g; Sodium: 599mg; Carbohydrates: 27g; Fiber: 14g; Sugars: 2g; Protein: 13g

Peanut Butter and Tahini Tofu Curry

UNDER 30 MINUTES

SERVES 4 · PREP TIME: 10 MINUTES · COOK TIME: 20 MINUTES

1 tablespoon olive oil

1 teaspoon dried garlic

1 teaspoon ground ginger

1 (15-ounce) package
    extra-firm tofu, cut into
    1-inch squares

¼ cup creamy
    peanut butter

2 tablespoons tahini

2 tablespoons low-sodium
    soy sauce

1 tablespoon distilled
    white vinegar

1 tablespoon sriracha

1 cup coconut milk from
    a carton

Salt

This fusion recipe brings together a medley of flavors in one dish. The combination of peanut butter and tahini is a perfect match for the tofu. It is a satisfying protein-rich entrée that is made easily.

1. In a skillet over medium heat, heat the olive oil. Add the garlic and ginger and stir for 10 seconds. Spread it evenly in one layer in the skillet.

2. Place the tofu pieces on top of the garlic-ginger mix. Cover the skillet and cook for 5 minutes.

3. Gently flip the tofu pieces, re-cover the skillet, and cook for 5 minutes more.

4. Reduce the heat to low. Using a spatula, gently stir in the peanut butter, tahini, soy sauce, vinegar, and sriracha, making sure the tofu is well covered with the sauce.

5. Turn the heat to medium. Add the coconut milk and gently mix. Re-cover the skillet and cook for 10 minutes.

6. Mix with a spatula, gently scraping the bottom of the skillet. Taste and season with salt. Serve over steamed rice or quinoa, as desired.

PER SERVING: Calories: 293; Total fat: 22g; Sodium: 644mg; Carbohydrates: 11g; Fiber: 3g; Sugars: 3g; Protein: 17g

Massaman Curry

GLUTEN-FREE, SOY-FREE

SERVES 4 · PREP TIME: 10 MINUTES · COOK TIME: 25 MINUTES

1 tablespoon olive oil

1 tablespoon dried garlic

1 tablespoon
ground ginger

1 teaspoon ground nutmeg

2 teaspoons ground
coriander

2 Yukon Gold potatoes,
peeled and chopped
into 1-inch pieces

2 cups unsweetened
coconut milk from
a carton

2 tablespoons creamy
peanut butter

2 teaspoons freshly
squeezed lemon juice

2 teaspoons light brown
sugar, plus more
as needed

1 teaspoon salt, plus more
as needed

Freshly ground
black pepper

A combination of Malaysian and Indian cuisine, massaman curry is made with potatoes cooked in peanut sauce along with Indian spices. I think it tastes heavenly when it's eaten straight out of a pot, so it's hard for me to hold back when I make this for my family. Pair it with whole-wheat flat bread and devour.

1. In a stockpot over high heat, heat the olive oil. Reduce the heat to low. Add the garlic, ginger, nutmeg, and coriander. Stir to combine. Add the potatoes and stir to combine.

2. Turn the heat to high. Stir in the coconut milk, peanut butter, lemon juice, brown sugar, and salt to combine. Cover the pot and cook for about 20 minutes, stirring every 5 minutes, until the potatoes are soft.

3. Taste and add more salt, pepper, or brown sugar, as needed.

Variation Tip: To give this dish a protein boost, at the start of cooking, lightly brown some extra-firm tofu cubes in sesame oil and add it to the dish during the last few minutes of cooking.

PER SERVING: Calories: 170; Total fat: 10g; Sodium: 628mg; Carbohydrates: 20g; Fiber: 3g; Sugars: 4g; Protein: 5g

Creamy Curried Lentils

GLUTEN-FREE, UNDER 30 MINUTES

SERVES 4 · PREP TIME: 10 MINUTES · COOK TIME: 20 MINUTES

2 teaspoons vegan butter

1 bay leaf

1 tablespoon cumin seeds

1 teaspoon minced garlic

½ cup finely chopped onion

1 cup red lentils, rinsed

2 teaspoons curry powder

1 teaspoon salt

½ cup unsweetened coconut cream

Lentils are a staple in any vegan diet because they are versatile enough to be cooked in a number of ways and adapt to a wide variety of cuisines. Here, the combination of lentils with spices and coconut cream is especially good.

1. On an electric pressure cooker, select sauté mode. Add the butter to melt. Add the bay leaf, cumin seeds, and garlic. Sauté for 1 minute. Add the onion and sauté for 2 minutes.

2. Stir in the lentils and curry powder.

3. Add the salt and 4 cups water and stir to combine. Cancel sauté mode. Close the lid and seal the valve. Pressure cook at high pressure for 10 minutes.

4. Carefully release the pressure, open the lid, and stir in the coconut cream. Serve hot over steamed rice or quinoa, as desired.

Cooking Tip: You can also make this on the stovetop in a stockpot or a Dutch oven by sautéing the ingredients following the same instructions. Cover and cook over medium-low heat until the lentils are soft, 20 to 30 minutes.

PER SERVING: Calories: 202; Total fat: 10g; Sodium: 616mg; Carbohydrates: 27g; Fiber: 9g; Sugars: 2g; Protein: 10g

Air Fryer Creole Vegetables

GLUTEN-FREE, NUT-FREE, SOY-FREE, UNDER 30 MINUTES

SERVES 4 · PREP TIME: 10 MINUTES · COOK TIME: 15 MINUTES

1 sweet potato, peeled and
   cut into slices
1 white onion, cut into
   2-inch squares
10 asparagus spears,
   woody ends trimmed
2 cups sliced baby bella
   mushrooms
1 cup (1-inch) cubed red
   bell pepper
5 garlic cloves, peeled
2 rosemary sprigs
1 teaspoon salt
2 tablespoons Creole
   seasoning
1 tablespoon olive oil

If you're craving crispy fried vegetables minus the grease, you really need an air fryer. The addition of fresh rosemary brings a wonderful aroma and flavor. Although I love to eat this as a lunchtime meal, it pairs well with rice to make a nice dinner.

1. Preheat an air fryer to 350°F.

2. In an air fryer basket, mix the sweet potato, onion, asparagus, mushrooms, red bell peppers, garlic, rosemary, salt, Creole seasoning, and olive oil.

3. Air fry for 15 minutes. Shake the basket and serve hot.

....

Cooking Tip: If you don't have an air fryer, bake the veggies on a 9-by-13-inch sheet pan in a 400°F oven for 20 minutes.

....

PER SERVING: Calories: 118; Total fat: 4g; Sodium: 591mg; Carbohydrates: 19g; Fiber: 5g; Sugars: 5g; Protein: 4g

Skillet Mediterranean Chickpeas

GLUTEN-FREE, NUT-FREE, SOY-FREE, UNDER 30 MINUTES

SERVES 4 · PREP TIME: 10 MINUTES · COOK TIME: 10 MINUTES

2 teaspoons olive oil

2 tablespoons chopped fresh parsley

1 tablespoon dried thyme

1 teaspoon minced garlic

1 teaspoon dried oregano

1 tablespoon tahini

1 (15-ounce) can chickpeas, drained and rinsed

½ cup vegetable broth

¼ cup sliced black olives

½ teaspoon salt

Pita bread, for serving (optional)

Lettuce leaves, for serving (optional)

Hummus, for serving (optional)

The neutral flavor of chickpeas makes them a wonderful addition to vegan dishes. I like to eat this dish as a salad and top it with dollops of hummus, whereas my husband loves to make a gyro wrap out of it.

1. In a skillet over medium-high heat, heat the olive oil. Add the parsley, thyme, garlic, and oregano. Sauté for about 1 minute until aromatic.

2. Stir in the tahini, mixing until the tahini paste loosens up.

3. Add the chickpeas, vegetable broth, olives, and salt. Stir to combine. Turn the heat to medium-low, cover the skillet, and cook for 5 minutes.

4. Using a spatula, mix well, scraping the bottom of the skillet. Serve, if desired, spooned into pita bread or lettuce leaves, and topped with a dollop of hummus.

Cooking Tip: You can make this in an electric pressure cooker set at high pressure for 10 minutes. Simply increase the vegetable broth to ¾ cup to keep the chickpeas from sticking to the vessel.

PER SERVING: Calories: 167; Total fat: 7g; Sodium: 426mg; Carbohydrates: 22g; Fiber: 6g; Sugars: <1g; Protein: 6g

Black Bean
Enchiladas, *page 87*

Chapter 6

Comfort Food Classics

Bolognese

SOY-FREE

SERVES 4 · PREP TIME: 10 MINUTES · COOK TIME: 30 MINUTES

8 ounces spaghetti
1 tablespoon olive oil
1 cup chopped onion
1 tablespoon minced garlic
½ cup julienned carrot
1 cup marinara
    sauce, divided
1 cup red lentils, rinsed
1 teaspoon salt
⅓ cup crushed walnuts

Just because you are vegan doesn't mean you can't eat Bolognese—at least when you make it with lentils and walnuts. These two ingredients provide the texture and taste of this much-loved Italian classic.

1. Bring a Dutch oven filled with water to a boil over high heat. Add the spaghetti and cook for 5 to 7 minutes until al dente. Drain and set aside.

2. Return the Dutch oven to high heat and add the olive oil to heat. Add the onion and garlic and sauté for 1 to 2 minutes until brown. Add the carrot and sauté for 1 minute more.

3. Turn the heat to medium. Stir in ½ cup of the marinara sauce and the lentils.

4. Stir in the salt and 2 cups water. Raise the heat to medium-high, cover the pot, and cook for 5 minutes. The lentils should be half done at this stage.

5. Stir in the walnuts. Re-cover the pot and cook for 1 minute. Stir to combine.

6. Turn the heat to medium. Add the remaining ½ cup of marinara sauce and ½ cup of water. Re-cover the pot and cook for 10 minutes. Stir to combine. The lentils should be soft but not mushy and most of the liquid should be absorbed. Serve over the cooked spaghetti.

PER SERVING: Calories: 465; Total fat: 14g; Sodium: 852mg; Carbohydrates: 75g; Fiber: 13g; Sugars: 8g; Protein: 19g

Black Bean Enchiladas

NUT-FREE

SERVES 4 · PREP TIME: 10 MINUTES · COOK TIME: 25 MINUTES

2 tablespoons olive oil

1 cup chopped onion

2 teaspoons dried garlic

2 teaspoons dried oregano

1 cup chopped tomato

1 zucchini, cut into
   ½-inch pieces

1 (15-ounce) can black
   beans, drained
   and rinsed

½ cup vegetable broth

1 teaspoon salt

4 (4-inch) corn tortillas

¾ cup shredded
   Mexican-style
   vegan cheese

Tabasco, for seasoning

After eating vegan enchiladas at Mexican restaurants, I decided to come up with my own nutritious version to make at home. In this recipe, black beans and zucchini bring plenty of fiber and protein, and the dish comes together easily.

1. Preheat the oven to 350°F.

2. In a Dutch oven over medium-high heat, heat the olive oil. Add the onion, garlic, and oregano. Sauté for about 2 minutes until translucent. Add the tomato and zucchini and sauté for 2 minutes more.

3. Stir in the black beans, vegetable broth, and salt. Cover the pot and cook for 2 minutes. Transfer half the black bean mixture to a small bowl.

4. Place the tortillas over the bean mixture in the Dutch oven. Top with the remaining black beans mixture. Sprinkle the cheese evenly over the tortillas.

5. Bake for 15 minutes, or until the cheese melts. Drizzle with Tabasco and enjoy.

Variation Tip: Cook the black bean filling in a skillet. Place the beans on each tortilla and roll them up. Place the rolls on a 9-by-13-inch sheet pan. Top with Enchilada Sauce (page 148) and shredded vegan cheese. Bake in a 350°F oven for 20 minutes, or until the cheese melts.

PER SERVING: Calories: 314; Total fat: 13g; Sodium: 888mg; Carbohydrates: 43g; Fiber: 9g; Sugars: 5g; Protein: 9g

Deconstructed Shepherd's Pie

GLUTEN-FREE, NUT-FREE, UNDER 30 MINUTES

SERVES 6 · PREP TIME: 10 MINUTES · COOK TIME: 20 MINUTES

1 tablespoon vegan butter

½ cup chopped onion

2 teaspoons dried thyme

2 cups (½-inch) cubed Yukon Gold potatoes

½ cup frozen green beans

½ cup frozen corn

1 tablespoon tomato paste

3 cups vegetable stock

1 cup red lentils, rinsed

1 teaspoon salt, plus more for seasoning

1 teaspoon freshly ground black pepper

This simplified shepherd's pie foregoes the traditional layered approach by mixing all the usual ingredients and mashing them together. You get all the flavor without all the fuss.

1. On an electric pressure cooker, select sauté mode. Add the butter to melt. Add the onion and thyme and sauté for about 1 minute until translucent.

2. Stir in the potatoes, green beans, and corn. Sauté, stirring continuously, for 2 minutes.

3. Stir in the tomato paste, mixing until it loosens and covers the vegetables.

4. Add the vegetable stock, lentils, salt, and pepper. Stir to combine. Cancel sauté mode. Close the lid and seal the valve. Pressure cook at high pressure for 10 minutes.

5. Carefully release the pressure and open the lid. With a food masher, mash the potatoes in the pressure cooker. (It's okay to mash the lentils along with the potatoes, but not too much). Taste and add more salt, as needed.

Cooking Tip: This recipe can be cooked in a stockpot or Dutch oven by following the same steps. Instead of pressure-cooking, cook, covered, over medium heat for about 20 minutes, or until potatoes and lentils are soft and can be mashed.

PER SERVING: Calories: 154; Total fat: 3g; Sodium: 713mg; Carbohydrates: 29g; Fiber: 8g; Sugars: 3g; Protein: 9g

Roasted Cauliflower Steak

GLUTEN-FREE, NUT-FREE, SOY-FREE, UNDER 30 MINUTES

SERVES 4 · PREP TIME: 10 MINUTES · COOK TIME: 20 MINUTES

2 heads cauliflower
1 teaspoon olive oil
1 teaspoon dried parsley
1 teaspoon dried thyme
1 teaspoon dried garlic
1 teaspoon dried oregano
1 teaspoon salt
½ teaspoon ground turmeric
½ teaspoon cayenne pepper

These cauliflower steaks are infused with an aromatic medley of herbs and are a beautiful color thanks to a little turmeric.

1. Preheat the oven to 400°F.

2. Cut off the cauliflower stems, then place the heads cut-side down and slice into ½-inch-thick steaks. Coat the steaks with olive oil and arrange on a 9-by-13-inch sheet pan in a single layer.

3. In a small bowl, stir together the parsley, thyme, garlic, oregano, salt, turmeric, and cayenne. Sprinkle the spice mixture over both sides of the cauliflower steaks.

4. Bake for about 20 minutes, flipping halfway using a spatula, until the cauliflower is tender and golden brown.

. . . .

Serving Suggestion: For those who like things spicy, drizzle some sriracha or your favorite hot sauce over the cauliflower.

. . . .

PER SERVING: Calories: 87; Total fat: 2g; Sodium: 669mg; Carbohydrates: 16g; Fiber: 8g; Sugars: 6g; Protein: 6g.

Turmeric Mac 'n' Cheese

UNDER 30 MINUTES

SERVES 6 · PREP TIME: 10 MINUTES · COOK TIME: 10 MINUTES

2½ cups elbow pasta

2 cups shredded vegan
    Cheddar cheese

½ cup unsweetened
    coconut milk from
    a carton

¼ cup nutritional yeast

1 tablespoon vegan butter

1 teaspoon salt

½ teaspoon ground
    turmeric

Freshly ground
    black pepper

Who doesn't like mac and cheese? This version is one of my favorites because it gets a bump of health benefits from the turmeric. It's the perfect weeknight comfort food when you don't want to spend a lot of time in the kitchen.

1. In a stockpot over high heat, stir together the pasta and 4 cups water. Bring to a boil. Cook for 7 to 8 minutes until al dente.

2. Turn the heat to low. Add the Cheddar cheese, coconut milk, nutritional yeast, butter, salt, and turmeric. Season with pepper. Stir until the cheese melts. Serve immediately.

Cooking Tip: The sauce in this will thicken if the dish is not served immediately or is stored for leftovers. Simply warm it and add more coconut milk until the desired consistency is reached.

PER SERVING: Calories: 316; Total fat: 12g; Sodium: 796mg; Carbohydrates: 44g; Fiber: 5g; Sugars: 2g; Protein: 8g

Carbonara

UNDER 30 MINUTES

SERVES 6 · PREP TIME: 10 MINUTES · COOK TIME: 10 MINUTES

1 (1-pound) package
　spaghetti
½ cup unsweetened
　coconut milk from
　a carton
½ cup nutritional yeast
½ cup chopped
　fresh parsley
2 tablespoons vegan butter
2 tablespoons tahini
2 teaspoons freshly ground
　black pepper
1 tablespoon freshly
　squeezed lemon juice
1½ teaspoons salt

If you're pressed for time, you can't go wrong with this 20-minute carbonara. It has all the familiar flavors of the original with the addition of tahini paste for an extra dimension of flavor.

1. Bring a Dutch oven filled with water to a boil over high heat. Add the spaghetti and cook for 5 to 7 minutes until al dente. Reserve ½ cup of cooking liquid in the Dutch oven and drain the rest of the liquid from the spaghetti, leaving the spaghetti in the pot.

2. Immediately add the coconut milk, nutritional yeast, parsley, butter, tahini, pepper, lemon juice, and salt to the spaghetti and toss with tongs until well combined. Serve immediately.

PER SERVING: Calories: 380; Total fat: 8g; Sodium: 637mg; Carbohydrates: 62g; Fiber: 4g; Sugars: 2g; Protein: 15g

Mushroom Stroganoff

NUT-FREE

SERVES 4 · PREP TIME: 10 MINUTES · COOK TIME: 30 MINUTES

2 tablespoons vegan butter

1 tablespoon minced garlic

2 teaspoons dried thyme

8 ounces baby bella
mushrooms, sliced

4 cups vegetable
broth, divided

1 cup unsweetened
coconut milk from
a carton

1 teaspoon salt

1 teaspoon freshly ground
black pepper

12 ounces fettuccine pasta

1 tablespoon unsweetened
coconut cream

I am a big mushroom fan. When they are nicely cooked in a creamy vegan base along with pasta it becomes my favorite go-to meal. To avoid pots to wash, I cook the mushrooms and pasta together in the same pan.

1. In a Dutch oven over high heat, melt the butter. Add the garlic and thyme and sauté for about 30 seconds until aromatic.

2. Turn the heat to medium-high. Add the mushrooms and cover the pot. Cook for 15 minutes. Mix thoroughly.

3. Turn the heat to high. Add 2 cups of the vegetable broth, the coconut milk, salt, and pepper. Stir to combine.

4. Add the fettuccine, making sure the pasta is completely submerged in the liquid, and cook for 2 to 3 minutes. Using tongs, toss the pasta to mix well.

5. Turn the heat to medium. Add 1 cup of the vegetable broth, re-cover the pot, and cook for 1 minute.

6. Stir in the coconut cream and mix well.

7. Turn the heat to low and add the remaining 1 cup of vegetable broth. Re-cover the pot and cook for 2 to 3 minutes. Toss with the tongs, remove from the heat, re-cover, and let sit for 2 minutes before serving.

PER SERVING: Calories: 403; Total fat: 9g; Sodium: 1,187mg; Carbohydrates: 70g; Fiber: 5g; Sugars: 4g; Protein: 13g

Boston Baked Beans

GLUTEN-FREE, NUT-FREE, SOY-FREE, UNDER 30 MINUTES

SERVES 4 • PREP TIME: 10 MINUTES • COOK TIME: 20 MINUTES

1 tablespoon olive oil

½ cup chopped onion

2 tablespoons tomato paste

1 (15-ounce) can navy beans, drained and rinsed

1½ cups vegetable broth

¼ cup molasses

2 tablespoons pure maple syrup

1 teaspoon salt

1 teaspoon freshly ground black pepper

½ teaspoon ground mustard

This vegan version of Boston baked beans forgoes the pork but retains that rich, slightly sweet and smoky flavor, thanks to molasses and maple syrup. It can be enjoyed in a bowl on its own or as a side dish to a bigger feast.

1. In a stockpot over high heat, heat the olive oil. Add the onion and sauté for about 1 minute until golden. Add the tomato paste and sauté for about 1 minute until it loosens up.

2. Stir in the navy beans.

3. Add the vegetable broth, molasses, maple syrup, salt, pepper, and mustard. Stir to combine. Cook for 10 to 15 minutes until the beans are tender.

PER SERVING: Calories: 233; Total fat: 4g; Sodium: 854mg; Carbohydrates: 44g; Fiber: 6g; Sugars: 25g; Protein: 7g

Sloppy Joes

NUT-FREE, SOY-FREE, UNDER 30 MINUTES

SERVES 4 • PREP TIME: 10 MINUTES • COOK TIME: 20 MINUTES

1 tablespoon olive oil

½ cup chopped onion, plus more for serving (optional)

½ cup chopped green bell pepper

2 tablespoons ketchup

1 tablespoon tomato paste

1 teaspoon light brown sugar

½ teaspoon cayenne pepper

1 cup green lentils, rinsed

2¼ cups vegetable broth

1 teaspoon salt

4 hamburger buns

½ onion, sliced (optional)

1 avocado, sliced, for serving (optional)

Chopped jalapeño pepper, for serving (optional)

This meatless version of the classic sandwich served in school cafeterias and at kitchen counters across the country can be whipped up in around 30 minutes using an electric pressure cooker. Green lentils are a great protein substitute and they taste great.

1. On an electric pressure cooker, select sauté mode. Add the olive oil to heat. Add the onion and sauté for about 2 minutes until golden. Add the green bell pepper and sauté for 1 minute.

2. Stir in the ketchup, tomato paste, brown sugar, and cayenne, mixing until the tomato paste loosens up.

3. Stir in the lentils, stirring until well covered with the tomato sauce mixture.

4. Add the vegetable broth and salt and stir to combine. Cancel sauté mode. Close the lid and seal the valve. Pressure cook at high pressure for 10 minutes.

5. Carefully release the pressure and open the lid. Stir and serve the sloppy Joe piled on burger buns with your favorite toppings, like chopped onion (if using), sliced avocado (if using), and jalapeño (if using).

Variation Tip: This makes a great filling for tacos. Fill corn or flour tortillas and top with sliced scallion and chopped tomato.

PER SERVING: Calories: 347; Total fat: 7g; Sodium: 1,188mg; Carbohydrates: 58g; Fiber: 18g; Sugars: 8g; Protein: 19g

Tofu Sofritas

GLUTEN-FREE, NUT-FREE, UNDER 30 MINUTES

SERVES 4 · PREP TIME: 10 MINUTES · COOK TIME: 10 MINUTES

1 tablespoon olive oil

½ cup chopped onion

1 teaspoon minced garlic

½ cup minced canned chipotle peppers in adobo sauce, liquid retained

1 teaspoon dried oregano

1 (1-pound) package extra-firm tofu, drained and pressed

½ teaspoon salt

Chipotle peppers in adobo sauce are the hero of this recipe, infusing plenty of smoky flavor to the tofu in this dish. You'll quickly find yourself craving this over takeout versions sold at restaurants.

1. In a skillet over high heat, heat the olive oil. Add the onion and garlic and sauté for about 2 minutes until golden.

2. Add the chipotle peppers, adobo sauce, and oregano and mix well.

3. Using your hands, crumble the tofu into the skillet and stir until it is covered with the sauce.

4. Add the salt and ¼ cup water and mix well. Cover the skillet and cook for about 5 minutes until the liquid is absorbed. Using a spatula, stir again, scraping the bottom of the skillet.

Serving Suggestion: Make this dish into a bowl by topping it with salsa, guacamole, lettuce, and some brown rice, or turn it into a burrito by folding it in a tortilla wrap.

PER SERVING: Calories: 167; Total fat: 10g; Sodium: 525mg; Carbohydrates: 9g; Fiber: 3g; Sugars: 3g; Protein: 12g

Flying Jacob

UNDER 30 MINUTES

SERVES 4 · PREP TIME: 10 MINUTES · COOK TIME: 20 MINUTES

1 (15-ounce) can
chickpeas, drained
and rinsed

1 large banana, cut
into slices

½ cup salted peanuts

2 tablespoons low-sodium
soy sauce

1 tablespoon ketchup

1 tablespoon sriracha

1 teaspoon curry powder

½ cup unsweetened
coconut cream

Salt

Cooked brown rice, for
serving (optional)

You may find yourself doing a double take when you read the ingredient list here, but Flying Jacob is a retro comfort classic that hails from Sweden. It's a fun and hassle-free meal that's especially popular with fussy young eaters. In this vegan version, you'll be surprised by how well the banana, chickpeas and peanuts go together. Give it a try!

1. Preheat the oven to 350°F.

2. On a 9-by-13-inch sheet pan, mix the chickpeas, bananas, peanuts, soy sauce, ketchup, sriracha, curry powder, and coconut cream. Spread the mixture into a single layer.

3. Bake for 20 minutes. Season with salt and serve immediately. Pair with brown rice (if using).

PER SERVING: Calories: 294; Total fat: 14g; Sodium: 607mg; Carbohydrates: 33g; Fiber: 8g; Sugars: 6g; Protein: 10g

Portobello Mushroom Pot Roast

NUT-FREE, UNDER 30 MINUTES

SERVES 6 · PREP TIME: 10 MINUTES · COOK TIME: 15 MINUTES

3 cups vegetable broth

2 tablespoons cornstarch

1 large Yukon Gold potato, cut into 1-inch pieces

2 (6-ounce) portobello mushrooms, cut into slices

½ cup chopped carrot

2 tablespoons low-sodium soy sauce

2 teaspoons dried thyme

1 teaspoon salt

1 teaspoon freshly ground black pepper

¼ teaspoon light brown sugar

Rich and flavorful portobello mushrooms have a wonderfully meaty texture and, when combined with potatoes and carrots, make a comforting pot "roast." Be sure to measure the ingredients carefully in this recipe to achieve its signature hearty texture.

1. In an electric pressure cooker, whisk the vegetable broth and cornstarch until smooth.

2. Add the potato, mushrooms, carrot, soy sauce, thyme, salt, pepper, and brown sugar. Using a spatula, stir to combine. Close the lid and seal the valve. Pressure cook at high pressure for 10 minutes.

3. Carefully release the pressure and open the lid.

Cooking Tip: This recipe can be made in a stockpot or Dutch oven. Instead of pressure cooking, cover the pot and let the ingredients cook over medium heat until the potatoes are soft and the mushrooms are chewy, about 30 minutes.

PER SERVING: Calories: 90; Total fat: 1g; Sodium: 1,015mg; Carbohydrates: 18g; Fiber: 3g; Sugars: 3g; Protein: 3g

Scalloped Potatoes

GLUTEN-FREE

SERVES 6 · PREP TIME: 10 MINUTES · COOK TIME: 40 MINUTES

2 tablespoons vegan butter

1 cup unsweetened
   almond milk

1 cup vegetable broth

2 teaspoons dried garlic

2 tablespoons cornstarch

¼ cup nutritional yeast

2 teaspoons paprika

1 teaspoon salt

1 teaspoon freshly ground
   black pepper

2 large Yukon Gold
   potatoes, cut into slices

Scalloped potatoes are always a hit in my home and this version has all the delicious creaminess of the classic dish using vegan butter, almond milk, and nutritional yeast.

1. Preheat the oven to 350°F.

2. In a Dutch oven over medium-high heat, melt the butter. Take the Dutch oven off the heat and add the almond milk, vegetable broth, and garlic. Immediately add the cornstarch and whisk until there are no lumps, about 3 minutes.

3. Return the Dutch oven to the stove and adjust the heat to medium. Stir in the nutritional yeast, paprika, salt, and pepper. Cook for 3 to 4 minutes until the mixture is hot but not boiling and starts to release steam.

4. Arrange the sliced potatoes in a single layer in the Dutch oven, making sure that every piece is covered by the gravy.

5. Bake for 30 minutes, or until the potatoes are soft and slightly golden.

Variation Tip: For a creamier scalloped potato dish, top the potatoes with ¼ cup cashew cream before placing it in the oven. For a cheesy flavor, top with 2 tablespoons grated vegan Parmesan.

PER SERVING: Calories: 167; Total fat: 7g; Sodium: 646mg; Carbohydrates: 23g; Fiber: 3g; Sugars: <1g; Protein: 4g

Lentil Goulash

NUT-FREE, SOY-FREE

SERVES 4 · PREP TIME: 10 MINUTES · COOK TIME: 35 MINUTES

1 tablespoon olive oil
½ cup chopped onion
1 bay leaf
1 cup chopped tomato
1 teaspoon paprika
1 cup green lentils, rinsed
4 cups vegetable broth
½ teaspoon salt
½ teaspoon freshly ground
    black pepper
½ cup macaroni pasta

Originating from Hungary, goulash became a popular dish on American dining tables, often with the addition of pasta. I've replaced the traditional meat with lentils, which produce a delicious and hearty stew with a hint of smokiness from the paprika.

1. On an electric pressure cooker, select sauté mode. Add the olive oil to heat. Add the onion and bay leaf and sauté for 2 to 3 minutes until golden.

2. Add the tomato and cook for about 2 minutes until mushy. Stir in the paprika.

3. Add the lentils and mix until they are well covered with the tomato mixture. Add the vegetable broth, salt, and pepper. Stir to combine. Cancel sauté mode. Close the lid and seal the valve. Pressure cook at high pressure for 10 minutes.

4. Carefully release the pressure and open the lid.

5. Select sauté mode again and add the macaroni. Cook for 5 to 7 minutes until the pasta is soft. Let rest for 2 to 3 minutes, or until the pasta is fluffy.

PER SERVING: Calories: 263; Total fat: 5g; Sodium: 832mg; Carbohydrates: 42g; Fiber: 15g; Sugars: 6g; Protein: 14g

Succotash

GLUTEN-FREE, NUT-FREE, SOY-FREE, UNDER 30 MINUTES

SERVES 4 · PREP TIME: 10 MINUTES · COOK TIME: 15 MINUTES

2 tablespoons olive oil

2 teaspoons dried garlic

1 teaspoon dried basil

1 teaspoon dried parsley

1 cup chopped onion

1 cup chopped tomato

1 (12-ounce) package frozen corn

1 (12-ounce) package frozen okra

1 teaspoon salt

1 teaspoon freshly ground black pepper

With roots in Native American cooking, succotash is a popular summer dish that showcases a bounty of vegetables. Quick and easy to make, it is naturally vegan and I love to make this recipe when I'm short on time.

1. In a skillet over high heat, heat the olive oil. Stir in the garlic, basil, and parsley.

2. Add the onion and sauté for 2 to 3 minutes until it starts to brown.

3. Add the tomato and cook for 2 minutes.

4. Turn the heat to medium-high. Stir in the corn, okra, salt, and pepper. Cover the skillet and cook for 5 to 7 minutes until the okra is soft. Stir to combine and serve hot.

....

Variation Tip: Succotash is a versatile dish that can be made using many types of vegetables, such as bell pepper, zucchini, squash, and lima beans, which are the most popular additions.

....

PER SERVING: Calories: 172; Total fat: 8g; Sodium: 593mg; Carbohydrates: 26g; Fiber: 5g; Sugars: 7g; Protein: 5g

Paprika Sweet Potato
Fries, *page 104*

Chapter 7

Snacks & Sides

Paprika Sweet Potato Fries

GLUTEN-FREE, NUT-FREE, SOY-FREE

SERVES 6 · PREP TIME: 10 MINUTES · COOK TIME: 30 MINUTES

2 large sweet potatoes, cut into ½-inch-thick slices
2 teaspoons olive oil
2 tablespoons cornstarch
1 teaspoon dried thyme
1 teaspoon salt
½ teaspoon paprika

Who doesn't love to indulge in a bowl of warm and crispy fries? Sweet potatoes pair perfectly with the smoky flavor of paprika in this oven-baked, guilt-free recipe.

1. Preheat the oven to 425°F. Line a 9-by-13-inch sheet pan with parchment paper.

2. On the prepared sheet pan, mix the sweet potatoes and olive oil to coat.

3. In a small bowl, whisk the cornstarch, thyme, salt, and paprika to combine. Sprinkle the mixture over the sweet potatoes and mix to combine thoroughly. Spread the sweet potatoes into an even layer on the sheet pan.

4. Bake for 30 minutes, or until crispy. Serve with your favorite condiment.

Serving Suggestion: The Lemon Garlic Butter Sauce (page 150) is a delicious accompaniment for these fries.

PER SERVING: Calories: 78; Total fat: 2g; Sodium: 401mg; Carbohydrates: 15g; Fiber: 2g; Sugars: 5g; Protein: 1g

Crispy Garlic Broccoli

GLUTEN-FREE, NUT-FREE, SOY-FREE, UNDER 30 MINUTES

SERVES 4 · PREP TIME: 10 MINUTES · COOK TIME: 12 MINUTES

4 cups broccoli florets
1 tablespoon olive oil
¼ cup nutritional yeast
2 tablespoons dried garlic
½ teaspoon salt
1 teaspoon freshly ground black pepper

Nothing short of a superfood, broccoli is loaded with fiber, vitamin C, and disease-fighting antioxidants. Air frying it with garlic turns it into a delicious and crunchy side or snack.

1. Preheat an air fryer to 350°F.

2. In a large bowl, mix the broccoli and olive oil until well coated.

3. Add the nutritional yeast, garlic, salt, and pepper. Mix well. Place the florets in the air fryer basket.

4. Cook for 10 to 12 minutes, or until crispy.

Cooking Tip: Don't have an air fryer? Place the seasoned broccoli florets on a 9-by-13-inch sheet pan and bake in a 400°F oven for 25 to 30 minutes until well done. They won't have the same crispiness as from the air fryer, but will still make a great side.

PER SERVING: Calories: 95; Total fat: 4g; Sodium: 312mg; Carbohydrates: 9g; Fiber: 4g; Sugars: 2g; Protein: 5g

Pan-Seared Maple Balsamic Brussels Sprouts

GLUTEN-FREE, NUT-FREE, SOY-FREE, UNDER 30 MINUTES

SERVES 4 · PREP TIME: 10 MINUTES · COOK TIME: 15 MINUTES

2 tablespoons olive oil

9 ounces Brussels
sprouts, halved

1 teaspoon dried garlic

3 tablespoons
balsamic vinegar

2 teaspoons pure
maple syrup

½ teaspoon salt

1 teaspoon freshly ground
black pepper

The rich flavors of balsamic and maple syrup blend beautifully with the nutritious crunch of Brussels sprouts. Even my kids love these!

1. In a skillet over high heat, heat the olive oil. Add the Brussels sprouts and garlic. Sauté for about 30 seconds until well coated with the oil.

2. Cover the skillet and cook for about 5 minutes until the Brussels sprouts start to brown. Remove the lid and cook, stirring frequently, for 5 minutes more.

3. Turn off the heat, add the vinegar, maple syrup, salt, and pepper. Cook, stirring, for about 1 minute. Remove from the heat and let sit for 1 minute more before serving.

PER SERVING: Calories: 116; Total fat: 7g; Sodium: 310mg; Carbohydrates: 11g; Fiber: 3g; Sugars: 4g; Protein: 2g

Buffalo Cauliflower Wings

NUT-FREE, UNDER 30 MINUTES

SERVES 4 · PREP TIME: 10 MINUTES · COOK TIME: 20 MINUTES

1 tablespoon tomato paste

1 tablespoon low-sodium soy sauce

2 teaspoons distilled white vinegar

1 teaspoon dried garlic

1 teaspoon salt

½ teaspoon cayenne pepper

½ teaspoon paprika

1 tablespoon all-purpose flour

4 cups cauliflower florets

These baked cauliflower wings are perfect for game day, a summer barbecue, or a tasty snack that won't leave you feeling weighed down. The spicy buffalo sauce is easy to make with just a few basic ingredients.

1. Preheat the oven to 425°F.

2. In a large bowl, stir together the tomato paste and ½ cup water until smooth.

3. Whisk in the soy sauce, vinegar, garlic, salt, cayenne, and paprika. Add the flour and whisk until smooth, 1 to 2 minutes.

4. Add the cauliflower florets and stir to combine. Pour the cauliflower onto a 9-by-13-inch sheet pan.

5. Bake for 15 to 20 minutes, or until the cauliflower is tender.

....

PER SERVING: Calories: 40; Total fat: <1g; Sodium: 864mg; Carbohydrates: 7g; Fiber: 1g; Sugars: 3g; Protein: 2g

Rosemary Baked Potatoes

GLUTEN-FREE, NUT-FREE, SOY-FREE

SERVES 6 • PREP TIME: 10 MINUTES • COOK TIME: 30 MINUTES

6 Yukon Gold potatoes,
    rinsed, patted dry, and
    pricked with a fork
2 tablespoons olive oil
1 tablespoon
    fresh rosemary
    leaves, chopped
1 teaspoon garlic powder
½ teaspoon salt
Freshly ground
    black pepper

An air fryer can quickly make delicious baked potatoes that are crunchy on the outside and fluffy in the middle. The addition of fresh rosemary adds an extra touch of delicious.

1. Preheat an air fryer to 380°F.

2. In a large bowl, mix the potatoes, olive oil, rosemary, garlic powder, and salt until the potatoes are well coated. Place the potatoes in the air fryer basket and pour any remaining oil over the potatoes. Season with pepper.

3. Air fry for 25 to 30 minutes until the potatoes are cooked through.

Cooking Tip: If you prefer, place the potatoes on a 9-by-13-inch sheet pan and bake in a 400°F oven for about 40 minutes, or until cooked through.

Serving Suggestion: Once the potatoes are cooked, press down on them with a food masher, lightly breaking them open. Top them with vegan sour cream and fresh chives or Spicy Queso (page 141).

PER SERVING: Calories: 152; Total fat: 5g; Sodium: 194mg; Carbohydrates: 26g; Fiber: 2g; Sugars: 1g; Protein: 3g

Tahini Mashed Cauliflower

GLUTEN-FREE, NUT-FREE, UNDER 30 MINUTES

SERVES 6 · PREP TIME: 5 MINUTES · COOK TIME: 15 MINUTES

**24 ounces
cauliflower florets**

2 tablespoons tahini

1 tablespoon vegan butter

1 teaspoon salt

**1 teaspoon freshly ground
black pepper**

1 teaspoon dried parsley

If you're looking for a low-carb substitute for mashed potatoes, this is it. The addition of tahini brings a lovely, slightly nutty flavor to this healthy side dish.

1. In an electric pressure cooker, stir together the cauliflower and ¾ cup water. Close the lid and seal the valve. Pressure cook at high pressure for 10 minutes.

2. Carefully release the pressure and open the lid. Using a food masher, mash the cauliflower in the pressure cooker.

3. Stir in the tahini, butter, salt, pepper, and parsley.

Variation Tip: For a creamier finish, top this with vegan butter. The Onion Mushroom Gravy (page 149) also makes a delicious topping for this dish.

PER SERVING: Calories: 91; Total fat: 6g; Sodium: 467mg; Carbohydrates: 7g; Fiber: 3g; Sugars: 3g; Protein: 4g

Miso-Glazed Tofu

NUT-FREE, UNDER 30 MINUTES

SERVES 4 · PREP TIME: 5 MINUTES · COOK TIME: 20 MINUTES

2 tablespoons sesame oil
¼ cup chopped scallion
¼ cup chopped celery
1 tablespoon miso paste
1 tablespoon low-sodium
**   soy sauce**
1 tablespoon pure
**   maple syrup**
½ tablespoon distilled
**   white vinegar**
½ teaspoon ground ginger
1 (15-ounce) package
**   extra-firm tofu, pressed,**
**   drained, and cut**
**   into slices**
1 tablespoon sesame seeds

Miso paste is primarily made from fermented soybean paste and is wonderfully salty in taste. When combined in this recipe with tofu, it creates a rich flavor known in Japanese as "umami."

1. In a skillet over high heat, heat the sesame oil. Add the scallion and celery and sauté for 1 minute.

2. Turn the heat to low. Whisk in the miso paste, soy sauce, maple syrup, vinegar, and ginger until well blended.

3. Adjust the heat to medium-low. Arrange the tofu slices in the skillet in a single layer and cook for 4 to 5 minutes until the tofu starts to brown.

4. Using a spatula, gently flip the tofu slices, making sure to scrape the marinade from the bottom of the skillet. Cook for 10 to 15 minutes more until the tofu is browned and slightly crispy.

5. Sprinkle the sesame seeds over the tofu and turn off the heat. Gently mix again without breaking the tofu slices and serve.

Cooking Tip: To make this a complete meal, serve it with quinoa and the Crispy Garlic Broccoli (page 105) or Skillet-Fried Eggplant (page 112). Top with the Peanut Satay Sauce (page 145).

PER SERVING: Calories: 200; Total fat: 13g; Sodium: 400mg; Carbohydrates: 10g; Fiber: 2g; Sugars: 3g; Protein: 12g

Corn Pudding

GLUTEN-FREE

SERVES 6 · PREP TIME: 5 MINUTES · COOK TIME: 3 HOURS

1½ **cups canned unsweetened coconut milk**

2 **tablespoons cornstarch**

3 **cups frozen corn**

½ **cup chopped onion**

¼ **cup nutritional yeast**

1 **tablespoon vegan butter**

1 **teaspoon salt**

1 **teaspoon freshly ground black pepper**

This is a savory corn pudding—basically a hybrid of corn casserole made with frozen corn kernels. It makes a creamy and satisfying side to vegetable-based mains.

1. In a slow cooker, whisk the coconut milk and cornstarch until smooth.

2. Add the corn, onion, nutritional yeast, butter, salt, and pepper, and stir to combine.

3. Cover the cooker and cook on high heat for 1 hour.

4. Stir the mixture, spread it out evenly, re-cover the cooker, and cook on high heat for 2 hours more.

....

Cooking Tip: This recipe can be cooked in the Dutch oven. Without warming it, stir together the milk and cornstarch. Then combine all the ingredients and turn the heat to high. Cover the pot and cook for 15 minutes. Stir nicely. Re-cover the pot and cook for 15 minutes, or until set and not runny.

....

PER SERVING: Calories: 232; Total fat: 13g; Sodium: 427mg; Carbohydrates: 26g; Fiber: 3g; Sugars: 4g; Protein: 6g

Skillet-Fried Eggplant

GLUTEN-FREE, NUT-FREE, SOY-FREE, UNDER 30 MINUTES

SERVES 4 • PREP TIME: 10 MINUTES • COOK TIME: 15 MINUTES

1 teaspoon salt

½ teaspoon chili powder

½ teaspoon ground turmeric

2 small eggplants, cut into long slices

2 tablespoons olive oil

Fried eggplant can sometimes turn out soggy. Here, it is lightly coated in oil for a healthier touch. Coupled with simple spices, it makes a great side that pairs well with rice.

1. In a small bowl, stir together the salt, chili powder, and turmeric. Rub each slice of eggplant with the spice mix.

2. In a skillet over medium heat, heat the olive oil.

3. Place the eggplant slices in the skillet and cook for 5 to 10 minutes until golden. Using a spatula, flip the eggplant and cook for 5 to 7 minutes more until golden on the second side.

PER SERVING: Calories: 133; Total fat: 8g; Sodium: 593mg; Carbohydrates: 17g; Fiber: 7g; Sugars: 10g; Protein: 3g

Sautéed Mushrooms

NUT-FREE, UNDER 30 MINUTES

SERVES 4 • PREP TIME: 10 MINUTES • COOK TIME: 15 MINUTES

2 tablespoons vegan butter

2 teaspoons dried garlic

8 ounces sliced baby bella mushrooms

2 tablespoons low-sodium soy sauce

1 teaspoon red pepper flakes

1 tablespoon dried parsley

Salt

Ready in just 25 minutes, these juicy sautéed mushrooms are the perfect go-to when you need a quick and easy side dish.

1. In a skillet over high heat, melt the butter. Add the garlic and mushrooms. Sauté for about 2 minutes until the mushrooms are well coated with butter.

2. Stir in the soy sauce, red pepper flakes, and parsley to combine. Turn the heat to medium, cover the skillet, and cook for 5 to 10 minutes until the mushrooms are browned. Stir, taste, and season with salt.

Cooking Tip: These are great served with toast for breakfast, tossed with some pasta and a squeeze of lemon juice, or as a versatile dinner-table side.

PER SERVING: Calories: 74; Total fat: 6g; Sodium: 522mg; Carbohydrates: 4g; Fiber: 1g; Sugars: 1g; Protein: 3g

Caramelized Green Beans with Sesame Seeds

NUT-FREE, UNDER 30 MINUTES

SERVES 4 · PREP TIME: 5 MINUTES · COOK TIME: 20 MINUTES

2 tablespoons olive oil

**1 (12-ounce) package
    frozen green beans**

**2 tablespoons low-sodium
    soy sauce**

1 tablespoon sesame seeds

**1 teaspoon pure
    maple syrup**

Salt

**Freshly ground
    black pepper**

This recipe elevates green beans from a humble side to star attraction. Soy sauce and maple syrup bring a nicely contrasting savory and sweet flavor profile, and caramelizing the beans produces a richer finish. If you prefer, you can cook these in a skillet with a lid to achieve the same result.

1. In a Dutch oven over high heat, heat the olive oil.

2. Turn the heat to medium. Add the green beans and cover the pot. Cook for 5 to 7 minutes until the beans soften a bit.

3. Stir in the soy sauce, sesame seeds, and maple syrup. Re-cover the pot and cook for about 10 minutes more until well done. The beans should be cooked thoroughly, soft and chewy, but should not change color. Taste and season with salt and pepper, mix again, and serve hot.

PER SERVING: Calories: 95; Total fat: 8g; Sodium: 451mg; Carbohydrates: 4g; Fiber: 1g; Sugars: 2g; Protein: 1g

Roasted Cabbage Wedges with Chive Vinaigrette

GLUTEN-FREE, NUT-FREE, SOY-FREE

SERVES 6 · PREP TIME: 10 MINUTES · COOK TIME: 30 MINUTES

1 head cabbage, trimmed and cut into 8 wedges

2 tablespoons olive oil

¼ cup chopped fresh chives

¼ cup balsamic vinegar

⅛ teaspoon ground mustard

Salt

Freshly ground black pepper

Since the time I discovered I can roast cabbage and it tastes fantastic as a result, this has become my favorite way to enjoy this veggie. When it comes out of the oven it smells tempting and the vinaigrette enhances the flavors with its sweet, tangy, and slightly salty deliciousness.

1. Preheat the oven to 400°F.

2. Place the cabbage wedges on a 9-by-13-inch sheet pan and drizzle them with olive oil, making sure each wedge is well coated.

3. Bake for 30 minutes, or until browned.

4. In a small bowl, whisk the chives, vinegar, and mustard until smooth. Drizzle the vinaigrette over the cabbage wedges and season with salt and pepper.

PER SERVING: Calories: 84; Total fat: 5g; Sodium: 31mg; Carbohydrates: 10g; Fiber: 4g; Sugars: 5g; Protein: 2g

Sautéed Butternut Squash

GLUTEN-FREE, NUT-FREE, SOY-FREE, UNDER 30 MINUTES

SERVES 4 · PREP TIME: 10 MINUTES · COOK TIME: 20 MINUTES

2 tablespoons olive oil

1 teaspoon ground ginger

1 teaspoon dried oregano

2 cups (1-inch) cubed butternut squash

1 teaspoon salt

1 tablespoon freshly squeezed lemon juice

This recipe makes a great side dish or, as I love to eat it, a flavorful healthy snack all by itself. I usually make a big batch to refrigerate (it will keep for up to 5 days) to heat and enjoy whenever hunger strikes.

1. In a skillet over high heat, heat the olive oil. Add the ginger and oregano and sauté for 10 seconds.

2. Add the squash and salt and stir to combine. Turn the heat to medium-high and cook for about 10 minutes until the squash starts to brown. Using a spatula, flip the squash and cook for 5 minutes more.

3. Stir in the lemon juice and serve hot.

PER SERVING: Calories: 105; Total fat: 7g; Sodium: 587mg; Carbohydrates: 12g; Fiber: 3g; Sugars: 2g; Protein: 1g

Air-Fried Stuffed Acorn Squash

NUT-FREE, UNDER 30 MINUTES

SERVES 4 · PREP TIME: 10 MINUTES · COOK TIME: 15 MINUTES

2 acorn squash, halved, seeded, and flesh scored

1 (15-ounce) can chickpeas, drained and rinsed

2 tablespoons low-sodium soy sauce

1 teaspoon dried garlic

1 teaspoon ground ginger

½ teaspoon ground cumin

2 tablespoons chopped scallion

Salt

Every fall I love to roast acorn squash with chickpeas. By using an air fryer, you can achieve the same texture as oven-roasted squash without any oil. The chickpeas in this recipe come out nice and crispy on top and, combined with the mild and sweet flavor of the squash, offer lip-smacking results.

1. Preheat an air fryer to 400°F.

2. Place the squash halves in the air fryer basket, cut-side up.

3. In a large bowl, stir together the chickpeas, soy sauce, garlic, ginger, cumin, and scallion. Spoon the mixture into the scored acorn squash halves. Season with salt and attach the basket to the air fryer.

4. Air fry for 15 minutes. The acorn squash should be soft when pricked with a fork. Serve immediately.

PER SERVING: Calories: 201; Total fat: 1g; Sodium: 458mg; Carbohydrates: 44g; Fiber: 9g; Sugars: <1g; Protein: 8g

Oven-Roasted Sesame Asparagus

NUT-FREE

SERVES 4 · PREP TIME: 5 MINUTES · COOK TIME: 30 MINUTES

2 tablespoons low-sodium
   soy sauce

1 teaspoon distilled
   white vinegar

1 teaspoon ground ginger

1 teaspoon pure
   maple syrup

½ teaspoon freshly ground
   black pepper

12 ounces
   asparagus spears

1 tablespoon sesame seeds

Salt

After going vegan, asparagus quickly became one of my favorite greens. Although it is often served seared or steamed, I've discovered that roasting asparagus in the oven with a glaze and some sesame seeds results in a lovely texture and taste.

1. Preheat the oven to 400°F.

2. In a large bowl, whisk the soy sauce, vinegar, ginger, maple syrup, and pepper to combine.

3. Add the asparagus and toss to coat in the soy sauce mixture. Arrange the spears in a single layer on a 9-by-13-inch sheet pan. Sprinkle with the sesame seeds.

4. Bake for 25 to 30 minutes, or until tender. Season with salt.

PER SERVING: Calories: 43; Total fat: 1g; Sodium: 453mg; Carbohydrates: 7g; Fiber: 2g; Sugars: 3g; Protein: 3g

Creamed Tofu and Spinach

GLUTEN-FREE

SERVES 4 · PREP TIME: 10 MINUTES · COOK TIME: 15 MINUTES · REST TIME: 15 MINUTES

8 ounces extra-firm tofu

1 cup canned unsweetened coconut milk

2 tablespoons cornstarch

1 tablespoon vegan butter

2 cups chopped fresh baby spinach

¼ cup nutritional yeast

1 teaspoon garlic powder

1 teaspoon salt

1 teaspoon freshly ground black pepper

¼ teaspoon ground turmeric

This recipe offers a hearty take on classic creamed spinach. Who needs dairy when tofu brings a lovely smooth texture to the dish while also packing in plenty of extra protein?

1. In a blender, blend the tofu until smooth. Set aside.

2. In a Dutch oven, whisk the coconut milk and cornstarch until smooth. Place the pot over medium heat and add the butter to melt, stirring for about 10 seconds.

3. Turn the heat to low. Add the spinach, nutritional yeast, garlic, salt, and pepper. Stir well.

4. Stir in the blended tofu and turmeric until well mixed. Spread the mixture in the Dutch oven in an even layer. Cover the pot and cook for 10 minutes. Turn off the heat and let rest, covered, for 15 minutes more.

PER SERVING: Calories: 229; Total fat: 16g; Sodium: 661mg; Carbohydrates: 11g; Fiber: 2g; Sugars: 1g; Protein: 10g

Banana Cream
Cheese Spring Rolls,
page 127

Chapter 8

Desserts

Air-Fryer Baked Apples

GLUTEN-FREE, SOY-FREE, UNDER 30 MINUTES

SERVES 4 · PREP TIME: 10 MINUTES · COOK TIME: 15 MINUTES

½ cup chopped walnuts

½ cup packed light
brown sugar

¼ cup dried cranberries

½ teaspoon ground
cinnamon

½ teaspoon
ground nutmeg

¼ teaspoon ground
cardamom

4 Red Delicious or
Gala apples

Vegan ice cream, for
serving (optional)

These baked apples are made even simpler with the help of an air fryer, which achieves the same effect as an oven in half the time. The natural flavor of fresh juicy apples marries with aromatic spices and sweetness from the brown sugar for a decadent yet wholesome treat that is elegant enough to serve at a dinner party.

1. Preheat an air fryer to 350°F.

2. In a small bowl, stir together the walnuts, brown sugar, cranberries, cinnamon, nutmeg, and cardamom. Set aside.

3. Cut just the tops off the apples. With a paring knife, remove the core, making sure to keep the bottom of the apples intact. Place the apples in an air fryer basket with the opening facing up.

4. Stuff the apples with the filling, pushing it down with your fingers to get in as much as possible.

5. Air fry for 15 minutes. Serve with your favorite vegan ice cream (if using).

Cooking Tip: If you don't have an air fryer, place the stuffed apples in a 9-by-13-inch baking dish and bake them in a 375°F oven for 30 minutes.

PER SERVING: Calories: 298; Total fat: 10g; Sodium: 12mg; Carbohydrates: 64g; Fiber: 5g; Sugars: 46g; Protein: 3g

Coconut Rice Pudding

GLUTEN-FREE, SOY-FREE

SERVES 6 · PREP TIME: 10 MINUTES · COOK TIME: 50 MINUTES

1 tablespoon olive oil

¾ cup packed light brown sugar

¼ cup unsweetened coconut flakes

1 teaspoon ground cardamom

6 cups unsweetened coconut milk from a carton

½ cup white basmati rice, or long-grain white rice, rinsed

1 tablespoon crushed raw almonds

For this simple and satisfying dessert, rice and coconut flakes are simmered in aromatic cardamom and coconut milk. Although rice pudding is common in many cuisines around the world, the use of cardamom in this recipe gives a nod to the traditional Indian version, *kheer.*

1. In a stockpot over medium heat, heat the olive oil. Add the brown sugar, coconut flakes, and cardamom. Sauté for about 2 minutes until the sugar starts to melt.

2. While stirring to avoid crystalizing the sugar, quickly pour in the coconut milk. It may stick but don't worry, just keep stirring until the sugar dissolves.

3. Add the rice and bring the pudding to a boil, stirring frequently. Turn the heat to low and cook for about 45 minutes, stirring frequently, until the rice is tender.

4. Add the crushed almonds. Cook, stirring, for 2 minutes.

5. Let the pudding rest for 1 to 2 minutes. Serve warm or refrigerate and enjoy it cold later.

PER SERVING: Calories: 248; Total fat: 9g; Sodium: 28mg; Carbohydrates: 52g; Fiber: 2g; Sugars: 28g; Protein: 2g

Chocolate Brownie Cookies

NUT-FREE

MAKES 16 · PREP TIME: 20 MINUTES · COOK TIME: 15 MINUTES · REST TIME: 1 HOUR

1 tablespoon flax meal

¾ cup packed light
   brown sugar

¼ cup vegan butter

1 tablespoon
   vanilla extract

½ cup vegan mini
   chocolate chips, divided

½ cup all-purpose flour

½ cup buckwheat flour

2 tablespoons
   unsweetened
   cocoa powder

2 teaspoons baking powder

¼ teaspoon salt

These soft, fudgy cookies are always a hit in my home. My family even loves to gorge on the raw dough! Make sure to follow the recipe carefully because every step is important to achieve the right texture and flavor.

1. In a small bowl, stir together the flax meal and 3 tablespoons water. Set aside.

2. In a large bowl, using a wooden spoon, beat the brown sugar and butter for 1 to 2 minutes until smooth.

3. Add the vanilla and flax meal and beat with a spatula for about 5 minutes until light and fluffy.

4. In a microwave-safe bowl, microwave ¼ cup of chocolate chips on high power for 1 minute. Stir until completely melted and smooth. Add the melted chocolate to the sugar mixture and beat for 2 to 3 minutes until the batter is light and fluffy.

5. In another large bowl, whisk the all-purpose flour, buckwheat flour, cocoa powder, baking powder, and salt to combine.

6. Pour the wet ingredients into the flour mixture along with the remaining ¼ cup of chocolate chips and mix with your hands until a soft dough forms. Wrap the dough in plastic wrap and refrigerate for at least 1 hour.

7. Preheat the oven to 350°F. Line a 9-by-13-inch sheet pan with parchment paper.

8. Remove the dough from the refrigerator. It will be very firm. Divide the dough into 16 portions and roll each into a 1-inch ball. Place the dough balls on the prepared sheet pan ½-inch apart. Gently flatten the balls by pressing down on them with your palm.

9. Bake for 15 minutes. Let cool on a wire rack for at least 1 minute. The cookies may look undone. Let cool completely to firm up. Serve warm or at room temperature. Store leftovers in an airtight container at room temperature for up to 1 week.

. . . .

Cooking Tip: If you have an air fryer, fry the cookies at 300°F for 5 minutes.

. . . .

PER SERVING (1 COOKIE): Calories: 121; Total fat: 5g; Sodium: 132mg; Carbohydrates: 23g; Fiber: 1g; Sugars: 13g; Protein: 1g

Peanut Butter Chocolate Cake

GLUTEN-FREE

SERVES 6 · PREP TIME: 15 MINUTES · COOK TIME: 2 HOURS

Nonstick cooking spray
1 cup buckwheat flour
1 tablespoon unsweetened
    cocoa powder
1 teaspoon baking powder
½ teaspoon salt
2 large bananas
¾ cup pure maple syrup
½ cup creamy
    peanut butter
2 tablespoons olive oil
1 teaspoon vanilla extract
½ cup vegan mini
    chocolate chips
½ cup unsweetened
    almond milk
Vegan ice cream, for
    serving (optional)
Chocolate syrup, for
    serving (optional)

Not only does this cake pair chocolate and peanut butter to delicious effect, but also the use of buckwheat flour makes it a gluten-free affair. It's a whole-grain flour that is easy to work with and binds excellently, making it a great substitute to refined alternatives while sneaking in some extra protein, fiber, and vitamins.

1. Coat a slow cooker with cooking spray.

2. In a large bowl, using a wooden spoon, stir together the flour, cocoa powder, baking powder, and salt until there are no lumps.

3. In a medium bowl, mash the bananas. Whisk in the maple syrup, peanut butter, olive oil, and vanilla, whisking for about 2 minutes, until no lumps remain. Add the banana mixture to the flour mixture and stir to combine.

4. Fold in the chocolate chips. Stir in the almond milk until combined. Pour the batter into the slow cooker and gently shake the inner pot to spread the batter evenly.

5. Cover the cooker and cook on high heat for 2 hours, or until a toothpick inserted into the center comes out clean.

6. Enjoy warm or at room temperature, with vegan vanilla ice cream (if using) and chocolate syrup (if using).

PER SERVING: Calories: 477; Total fat: 22g; Sodium: 392mg; Carbohydrates: 68g; Fiber: 7g; Sugars: 44g; Protein: 10g

Banana Cream Cheese Spring Rolls

NUT-FREE, UNDER 30 MINUTES

SERVES 4 · PREP TIME: 15 MINUTES · COOK TIME: 10 MINUTES

1 large banana, mashed

¼ cup vegan cream cheese

2 tablespoons light brown sugar

1 teaspoon vanilla extract

4 spring roll wrappers, thawed if frozen

Although you'll be hard pressed to find anything more indulgent than these banana cream cheese spring rolls, they are much lighter than their deep-fried cousin because I use an air fryer, which cooks them to golden perfection—minus the oil.

1. Preheat an air fryer to 300°F.

2. In a medium bowl, stir together the mashed banana, cream cheese, brown sugar, and vanilla until creamy.

3. On a clean work surface, lay out the spring roll wrappers and cut them in half. Spread 1 to 2 tablespoons of the banana mixture on each spring roll half sheet, leaving the edges clear. Roll up each sheet and seal the edges using a little water.

4. Place the spring rolls in an air fryer basket and fry for 10 minutes. Serve hot.

Cooking Tip: These can also be made on a 9-by-13-inch sheet pan. Follow the recipe as instructed and bake in a 400°F oven for 15 minutes, or until they start to brown.

PER SERVING: Calories: 129; Total fat: 4g; Sodium: 77mg; Carbohydrates: 22g; Fiber: 2g; Sugars: 9g; Protein: 3g

Mixed Fruit Crisp

GLUTEN-FREE, SOY-FREE

SERVES 6 · PREP TIME: 10 MINUTES · COOK TIME: 30 MINUTES

1 cup frozen peaches

1 cup frozen raspberries

1 large apple, cut into slices

½ teaspoon ground cinnamon

1 teaspoon vanilla extract

1 cup old-fashioned oats

¼ cup almond flour

¼ cup packed light brown sugar

Vegan ice cream, for serving (optional)

This simple and guilt-free fruit crisp is great all year long. An extremely versatile dish, once you have mastered the (easy!) technique, you can use just about any fruit to make the filling, including apple, pear, rhubarb, or cherry.

1. Preheat the oven to 375°F.

2. On a 9-by-13-inch sheet pan, mix the peaches, raspberries, apple, cinnamon, and vanilla, spreading the fruit into a single layer.

3. Sprinkle the oats evenly over the fruit mixture. Then, sprinkle the almond flour evenly over the oats. Top with the brown sugar.

4. Bake for 30 minutes until golden brown.

5. Serve warm with your favorite vegan ice cream (if using).

Serving Suggestion: I like to make a big batch of this and refrigerate leftovers for 3 to 4 days to enjoy at breakfast for a fruit-filled start to the day. Spoon into a bowl and top with your favorite vegan milk or yogurt.

PER SERVING: Calories: 152; Total fat: 3g; Sodium: 4mg; Carbohydrates: 32g; Fiber: 5g; Sugars: 16g; Protein: 3g

Mango Sticky Rice

GLUTEN-FREE, SOY-FREE

SERVES 6 · PREP TIME: 10 MINUTES · COOK TIME: 30 MINUTES

2 cups canned unsweetened coconut milk

½ teaspoon ground cardamom

¼ cup powdered sugar

1 cup premium-quality sweet rice

1 cup frozen mango chunks

Although sticky rice is usually made in a steamer, I came up with this easy stovetop version that only requires a stockpot. Buy premium-quality sweet rice for the most delicious result.

1. In a stockpot, stir together the coconut milk, cardamom, powdered sugar, and ½ cup water.

2. Rinse the sweet rice thoroughly under warm water for about 2 minutes. It will start releasing its starch. Immediately add the rice to the stockpot. Place the pot over high heat and cook, stirring continuously, for about 5 minutes until the liquid starts to thicken.

3. Turn the heat to low, cover the pot, and cook for 15 to 20 minutes until the liquid is absorbed. Stir, making sure to scrape the bottom of the pot.

4. Add the mango, re-cover the pot, and turn off the heat. Let rest for 5 minutes. Mix again and serve at room temperature or cold.

PER SERVING: Calories: 290; Total fat: 15g; Sodium: 24mg; Carbohydrates: 35g; Fiber: 1g; Sugars: 9g; Protein: 4g

Key Lime Custard

GLUTEN-FREE, SOY-FREE

SERVES 6 · PREP TIME: 5 MINUTES · COOK TIME: 40 MINUTES

2 cups unsweetened almond milk
2 tablespoons cornstarch
¼ cup powdered sugar
1 tablespoon grated lime zest
1 teaspoon freshly squeezed lime juice

My mom always seemed to have a custard on hand as a treat for the kids or for unexpected guests when I was growing up. It's only recently that I realized just how easy it is to make, even without using dairy products. This key lime version is light and delicious over fresh fruit.

1. In a stockpot over high heat, cook the almond milk until hot but not boiling.

2. Turn the heat to low. Add the cornstarch and cook, whisking, for 1 to 2 minutes until there are no lumps.

3. Add the powdered sugar and whisk for about 30 seconds until it dissolves.

4. Raise the heat to medium and cook the custard for about 30 minutes, stirring frequently to prevent it from boiling over.

5. Turn off the heat. Without stirring, add the lime zest and lime juice and let the pot rest for 2 to 3 minutes. This will help avoid curdling. Quickly whisk the mixture for 10 seconds, cover the pot, and set aside for 10 minutes, or until it comes to room temperature.

6. Refrigerate in an airtight container until ready to serve. Spoon the custard over your favorite fruit, such as apples, bananas, or blueberries.

PER SERVING: Calories: 41; Total fat: 1g; Sodium: 57mg; Carbohydrates: 8g; Fiber: <1g; Sugars: 5g; Protein: <1g

Chocolate Mousse

GLUTEN-FREE, SOY-FREE

SERVES 4 • PREP TIME: 10 MINUTES • COOK TIME: 10 MINUTES • REST TIME: 2 HOURS

1 tablespoon flax meal

1 cup vegan mini chocolate chips

¾ cup unsweetened almond milk

¼ cup packed light brown sugar

1 teaspoon vanilla extract

2 teaspoons cornstarch

2 tablespoons unsweetened coconut cream

2 tablespoons shaved vegan chocolate

When I'm feeling stuck for dessert options to serve at home, I whip up this chocolate mousse. A rich and airy treat, it is loved by my daughter just as much as it by our grown-up guests.

1. In a small bowl, stir together the flax meal and 3 tablespoons water. Set aside.

2. In a stockpot over medium-high heat, combine the chocolate chips, almond milk, brown sugar, and vanilla. Cook for 1 to 2 minutes, whisking continuously until smooth, making sure the mixture doesn't boil.

3. Turn the heat to low. Add the cornstarch and cook, whisking until there are no lumps, about 1 minute.

4. Stir in the flax meal until well blended. Raise the heat to medium-high and cook for 3 to 4 minutes, whisking continuously, until the mixture starts to thicken.

5. Divide the mixture among 4 ramekins or small bowls and refrigerate for at least 2 hours. Just before serving, top with coconut cream and shaved chocolate.

Variation Tip: To change up the flavors a bit, sprinkle some chopped almonds or pistachios over the mousse, or a handful of fresh raspberries or cherries.

PER SERVING: Calories: 334; Total fat: 19g; Sodium: 45mg; Carbohydrates: 49g; Fiber: 3g; Sugars: 37g; Protein: 3g

Saffron Almond Fudge

GLUTEN-FREE, UNDER 30 MINUTES

SERVES 4 · PREP TIME: 10 MINUTES · COOK TIME: 20 MINUTES

2 teaspoons vegan butter

1 cup almond flour

¼ cup packed light brown sugar

¼ cup unsweetened almond milk

¼ teaspoon broken saffron threads

¼ teaspoon ground cardamom

This recipe is inspired by *badam halwa*, a traditional, fudge-like Indian sweet made from raw almonds that generally takes a long time to make. Here, I use almond flour instead of raw nuts to create a fuss-free (and much faster) fudge that tastes just as good as the original. Unlike American fudge, this treat is much softer and eaten with a spoon.

1. In a skillet over medium heat, melt the butter. Turn the heat to low. Add the almond flour and sauté for about 5 minutes until it becomes aromatic. Do not let it brown.

2. Stir in the brown sugar until well blended with the almond flour.

3. Add the almond milk, saffron, cardamom, and ¼ cup water. Stir to combine.

4. Adjust the heat to high and cook for 2 to 3 minutes, stirring continuously, until the liquid is absorbed.

5. Turn the heat to medium-low and cook for 5 minutes more, or until the mixture starts to change color and the saffron is aromatic. Turn off the heat. Cover the skillet, and let stand for 2 minutes. Spoon into bowls and serve hot.

PER SERVING: Calories: 231; Total fat: 16g; Sodium: 36mg; Carbohydrates: 25g; Fiber: 3g; Sugars: 14g; Protein: 6g

Peach-Pear Cobbler

SOY-FREE

SERVES 6 · PREP TIME: 15 MINUTES · COOK TIME: 40 MINUTES

2 cups sliced peaches

2 cups sliced pears

¼ cup pure maple syrup

2 teaspoons freshly squeezed lemon juice

1 teaspoon ground cinnamon

½ teaspoon ground ginger

1 cup whole-wheat flour

¼ cup packed light brown sugar

1 teaspoon baking powder

¼ teaspoon salt

1 cup unsweetened almond milk

Vegan vanilla ice cream, for serving (optional)

Plain dairy-free yogurt, for serving (optional)

Peaches and pears are topped with a quick batter that bakes to crispy perfection in this cobbler recipe. It is an especially warming dessert when the weather turns cold.

1. Preheat the oven to 400°F.

2. In a 9-by-13-inch sheet pan, mix the peaches, pears, maple syrup, lemon juice, cinnamon, and ginger until combined.

3. In a medium bowl, whisk the flour, brown sugar, baking powder, and salt until there are no lumps. Add the almond milk and whisk until a sticky doughlike batter forms. Using a spoon or cookie scoop, drop spoonfuls of the batter over the fruit, trying to cover the fruit as much as possible.

4. Bake for 35 to 40 minutes, or until the top is golden brown.

5. Serve warm with vegan vanilla ice cream (if using) or yogurt (if using).

PER SERVING: Calories: 194; Total fat: 1g; Sodium: 212mg; Carbohydrates: 50g; Fiber: 6g; Sugars: 27g; Protein: 3g

Pumpkin Pie Crumble

GLUTEN-FREE, SOY-FREE

SERVES 6 · PREP TIME: 15 MINUTES · COOK TIME: 3 HOURS

Nonstick cooking spray

3 tablespoons warm water

1 tablespoon chia seeds

1 (15-ounce) can pumpkin purée

½ cup unsweetened almond milk

¼ cup pure maple syrup

1 teaspoon pumpkin pie spice

½ cup old-fashioned oats

½ cup almond flour

¼ cup packed light brown sugar

2 tablespoons olive oil

Vegan vanilla ice cream, for serving (optional)

Vegan whipped cream, for serving (optional)

If you love the flavors of pumpkin pie, but want to skip the tricky pie-making process, then this hassle-free recipe is for you. I add chia seeds, which blend seamlessly with the flavor and texture, bringing extra nutritional value as a rich source of omega-3 fatty acids, fiber, and protein.

1. Coat a slow cooker with cooking spray.

2. In a small bowl, stir together the warm water and chia seeds. Let sit for 2 minutes.

3. In a large bowl, whisk the pumpkin purée, almond milk, maple syrup, soaked chia seeds, and pumpkin pie spice to blend. Pour the batter into the prepared slow cooker, smoothing it evenly with a spatula.

4. In another small bowl, whisk the oats, almond flour, and brown sugar until there are no lumps. Add the olive oil and mix with your hands until a crumbly texture forms. Spread the oat mixture evenly over the pumpkin mixture.

5. Cover the cooker and cook on high heat for 3 hours. Serve warm with vegan vanilla ice cream (if using) and vegan whipped cream (if using).

PER SERVING: Calories: 224; Total fat: 11g; Sodium: 22mg; Carbohydrates: 34g; Fiber: 6g; Sugars: 20g; Protein: 5g

Deconstructed Apple Pie

NUT-FREE

SERVES 6 • PREP TIME: 10 MINUTES • COOK TIME: 25 MINUTES

2 tablespoons vegan butter

5 cups apple slices

1 teaspoon ground cinnamon

½ teaspoon ground nutmeg

½ teaspoon ground cardamom

¾ cup pure maple syrup

½ cup all-purpose flour

½ teaspoon baking powder

⅛ teaspoon salt

Vegan whipped cream, for serving (optional)

This recipe takes the expression "as easy as apple pie" to a new level. You simply combine all the ingredients in a Dutch oven, cook, and voilà, an incredibly delicious dessert. No oven required.

1. In a Dutch oven over medium heat, melt the butter. Add the apples and sauté for 2 minutes, making sure they are well coated with butter.

2. Add the cinnamon, nutmeg, and cardamom and mix well. Cover the pot and cook for 3 or 4 minutes until aromatic.

3. Stir in the maple syrup. Turn the heat to medium-low, re-cover the pot, and cook for 10 minutes.

4. In a medium bowl, whisk the flour, baking powder, and salt to combine. Set aside.

5. Stir the apples once more and spread them into an even layer. Sprinkle the flour mixture evenly over the apples. Turn the heat to medium, re-cover the pot, and cook for 5 minutes. Stir the mixture to combine.

6. Serve warm, topped with vegan whipped cream (if using).

PER SERVING: Calories: 219; Total fat: 4g; Sodium: 110mg; Carbohydrates: 47g; Fiber: 3g; Sugars: 33g; Protein: 1g

Chocolate Soufflé

GLUTEN-FREE, NUT-FREE

SERVES 6 • PREP TIME: 20 MINUTES • COOK TIME: 15 MINUTES

Nonstick cooking spray
1 cup flax meal
2 tablespoons vegan butter
1 cup vegan mini chocolate chips
1 teaspoon baking powder
¼ teaspoon salt
¾ cup packed light brown sugar
1 tablespoon unsweetened cocoa powder

Soufflé is traditionally made from raw eggs, but this dairy-free version makes it a perfect fix when chocolate cravings strike.

1. Coat the inner pot of an electric pressure cooker with cooking spray.

2. In a large bowl, stir together the flax meal and 2½ cups water. Let sit for 5 minutes.

3. In a microwave-safe bowl, combine the butter and chocolate chips. Microwave on high power for 1 minute until melted. Stir until the chocolate is smooth and creamy.

4. To the flax meal, add the baking powder and salt and whisk until it has a gooey, eggy texture. Add the brown sugar and cocoa powder. Whisk for 3 to 4 minutes until a smooth batter forms.

5. Add the melted chocolate and whisk for 1 to 2 minutes until well blended. Pour the batter into the prepared pressure cooker. Close the lid and seal the valve. Pressure cook at high pressure for 10 minutes.

6. Carefully release the pressure and open the lid. Let sit for 2 minutes. Serve warm.

Variation Tip: Feeling extra decadent? Top the soufflé with vegan whipped cream, fresh berries, and a mint sprig.

PER SERVING: Calories: 371; Total fat: 20g; Sodium: 233mg; Carbohydrates: 61g; Fiber: 6g; Sugars: 42g; Protein: 5g

Easy One-Bowl Blondie

GLUTEN-FREE, SOY-FREE

SERVES 6 · PREP TIME: 10 MINUTES · COOK TIME: 40 MINUTES

2 large ripe
　bananas, mashed
½ cup pure maple syrup
2 tablespoons
　almond butter
1 tablespoon olive oil
½ cup almond flour
¼ cup chickpea flour
¼ cup flax meal
1 teaspoon baking powder
¼ teaspoon salt
¼ cup vegan mini
　chocolate chips

I love to make these blondies—not just for dessert but also as energy bars. They are more wholesome than the standard version thanks to the addition of bananas and maple syrup, which take the place of refined sugar. Chickpea flour adds protein and flax meal brings in some omega-3s.

1. Preheat the oven to 350°F. Line a 9-by-13-inch sheet pan with parchment paper. Set aside.

2. In a large bowl, whisk the mashed bananas, maple syrup, almond butter, and olive oil for 2 to 3 minutes until smooth.

3. Add the almond flour, chickpea flour, flax meal, baking powder, and salt. Whisk until thoroughly mixed. Pour the batter onto the center of the prepared sheet pan (do not spread it out to fill the sheet pan.) Gently smooth the top with a spatula without pressing it down. Sprinkle the chocolate chips evenly over the top.

4. Bake for 35 to 40 minutes, or until brown and a toothpick inserted into the center comes out clean. Let cool and cut into 12 squares. Store leftovers in an airtight container at room temperature for 4 to 5 days.

PER SERVING: Calories: 292; Total fat: 14g; Sodium: 183mg; Carbohydrates: 40g; Fiber: 5g; Sugars: 26g; Protein: 6g

Chapter 9

Staples & Sauces

Vegetable Broth

GLUTEN-FREE, NUT-FREE, SOY-FREE, UNDER 30 MINUTES

MAKES 5 CUPS · PREP TIME: 10 MINUTES · COOK TIME: 10 MINUTES

1¼ cups finely
   chopped carrot
1 cup finely chopped onion
1 celery stalk,
   finely chopped
1 rosemary sprig
2 tablespoons
   tomato paste
2 teaspoons dried basil
2 teaspoons dried parsley
1 teaspoon dried oregano
1 teaspoon salt

An electric pressure cooker makes the richest and most comforting broth in just minutes. You'll be surprised by the depth of flavor in this recipe even with its small ingredient list. Sip it as a flavorful, warming snack or use it as a base for a wide variety of soups, stews, and dishes like risotto.

1. In an electric pressure cooker, combine the carrot, onion, celery, rosemary, tomato paste, basil, parsley, oregano, salt, and 6 cups of water. Close the lid and seal the valve. Pressure cook at high pressure for 10 minutes.

2. Carefully release the pressure and open the lid. Using a food masher, roughly mash the vegetables.

3. Strain the broth into glass or plastic airtight containers and discard the solids. The broth will keep, refrigerated, for up to 1 month.

Cooking Tip: Make this on the stovetop. Combine the ingredients with 6 cups of water in a large pot over medium heat. Cover the pot and cook for 20 to 25 minutes, or until the ingredients are soft. Strain the broth into storage containers as directed.

PER 1-CUP SERVING: Calories: 36; Total fat: <1g; Sodium: 547mg; Carbohydrates: 8g; Fiber: 3g; Sugars: 4g; Protein: 1g

Spicy Queso

GLUTEN-FREE, SOY-FREE, UNDER 30 MINUTES

SERVES 4 · PREP TIME: 5 MINUTES · COOK TIME: 10 MINUTES

¼ **cup raw cashew nuts**

¼ **cup nutritional yeast**

1 tablespoon taco seasoning

1 canned chipotle pepper in adobo sauce

¼ **teaspoon ground turmeric**

Salt

Tortilla chips, for serving

Being vegan doesn't mean having to forgo queso with this wonderfully creamy cashew-based alternative. A great dip made quickly and with very few ingredients—once you taste it, it's hard to resist going back for more.

1. In a stockpot over high heat, bring 1 cup of water to a boil. Add the cashews, nutritional yeast, taco seasoning, chipotle pepper in adobo, and turmeric. Stir to combine. Turn off the heat. Let cool for 2 to 3 minutes.

2. Transfer the mixture to a high-speed blender and blend until smooth.

3. Taste and season with salt. Serve with tortilla chips.

....

Serving Suggestion: This queso pairs well with the Breakfast Burrito Casserole (page 24).

....

PER SERVING: Calories: 76; Total fat: 4g; Sodium: 260mg; Carbohydrates: 6g; Fiber: 2g; Sugars: 1g; Protein: 4g

Raspberry Chia Jam

GLUTEN-FREE, NUT-FREE, SOY-FREE

MAKES 1 CUP · PREP TIME: 5 MINUTES · COOK TIME: 15 MINUTES · REST TIME: 2 HOURS

1 (6-ounce) package fresh raspberries
½ cup pure maple syrup
½ teaspoon ground ginger
1 tablespoon chia seeds

This recipe combines the deliciousness of raspberry jam with the healthy goodness of chia seeds, which are a rich source of fiber, antioxidants, and omega-3 fatty acids. They absorb more than 10 times their weight in liquid, creating the perfect texture for this jam.

1. In a stockpot over high heat, stir together the raspberries, maple syrup, ginger, and chia seeds. Cook for 3 to 4 minutes until the raspberries are soft.

2. Turn the heat to low. Using a food masher, mash the raspberries in the pot.

3. Raise the heat to medium and cook for 2 minutes until the sauce starts to thicken. Let cool for 5 minutes to bring the jam to room temperature. Transfer to an airtight container and refrigerate for at least 2 hours before serving. The jam will keep, refrigerated, for up to 1 month.

Cooking Tip: This jam is a great way to sweeten up your morning granola and yogurt, breakfast toast, favorite muffin, or weekend pancakes.

PER ¼-CUP SERVING: Calories: 138; Total fat: 1g; Sodium: 4mg; Carbohydrates: 32g; Fiber: 4g; Sugars: 26g; Protein: 1g

Easy Cranberry Butter

GLUTEN-FREE, NUT-FREE

**MAKES 2 CUPS · PREP TIME: 5 MINUTES · COOK TIME: 15 MINUTES ·
REST TIME: 1 HOUR**

**12 ounces fresh
   cranberries**
¼ cup vegan butter
¼ cup powdered sugar
**1 tablespoon
   vanilla extract**
⅛ teaspoon salt

This sweet-tart cranberry butter is an easy-to-make condiment that requires just five ingredients. It has a wonderfully bright color that makes a beautiful addition to the breakfast table.

1. In a Dutch oven over high heat, stir together the cranberries, butter, powdered sugar, vanilla, and salt, stirring until the butter melts. Cover the pot and cook for about 5 minutes until the cranberries are mushy.

2. Stir and let cool for 5 minutes. Transfer the mixture to a blender and blend until smooth. Spoon into an airtight container and refrigerate for 1 hour before serving. The butter will keep, refrigerated, for about 1 week.

PER ¼-CUP SERVING: Calories: 120; Total fat: 7g; Sodium: 107mg; Carbohydrates: 12g; Fiber: 3g; Sugars: 8g; Protein: <1g

Sweetened Condensed Milk

GLUTEN-FREE, SOY-FREE

MAKES ABOUT 1 CUP · PREP TIME: 5 MINUTES · COOK TIME: 1 HOUR, 10 MINUTES

1 (14-ounce) can coconut milk
2 tablespoons powdered sugar
1 teaspoon vanilla extract

Vegan sweetened condensed milk can be hard to come by in the grocery store. Thankfully, this dairy-free version is a cinch to cook at home! It makes a great substitute for regular condensed milk in dessert recipes. You may even need a little self-restraint to avoid eating it by the spoonful.

1. In a stockpot over high heat, stir together the coconut milk, powdered sugar, and vanilla, stirring until all the ingredients dissolve, about 30 seconds.

2. Turn the heat to medium-low and cook, stirring every 5 minutes, for about 1 hour.

3. Let cool for 10 minutes. Transfer to an airtight container and refrigerate for up to 1 week.

PER 1-CUP SERVING: Calories: 779; Total fat: 70g; Sodium: 101mg; Carbohydrates: 27g; Fiber: 0g; Sugars: 21g; Protein: 5g

Peanut Satay Sauce

UNDER 30 MINUTES

SERVES 4 · PREP TIME: 5 MINUTES · COOK TIME: 2 MINUTES

1 cup unsweetened coconut milk from a carton

½ cup creamy peanut butter

2 tablespoons low-sodium soy sauce

2 tablespoons packed light brown sugar

½ teaspoon ground ginger

½ teaspoon dried garlic

1½ tablespoons freshly squeezed lemon juice

½ teaspoon salt

Although the traditional Thai rendition of satay sauce calls for crushing peanuts into a paste and grinding your own spices, this version takes a shortcut with a jar of peanut butter and a handful of pantry basics. You get the same rich and creamy flavor, but it takes less than 10 minutes to make!

1. In a stockpot over medium-high heat, whisk the coconut milk, peanut butter, soy sauce, brown sugar, ginger, and garlic until smooth, 1 to 2 minutes. Bring the mixture to a boil, turn the heat to low, and continue whisking until the mixture starts to thicken.

2. Turn off the heat and whisk in the lemon juice and salt. Serve warm, at room temperature, or cold. Refrigerate leftovers in an airtight container for up to 2 weeks.

Serving Suggestion: This sauce is wonderful drizzled over noodles, spring rolls, or roasted vegetables. I love to pour it over the Miso-Glazed Tofu (page 110) and serve it with some quinoa for a complete meal.

PER SERVING: Calories: 234; Total fat: 17g; Sodium: 898mg; Carbohydrates: 17g; Fiber: 2g; Sugars: 11g; Protein: 9g

Easy Butterscotch

GLUTEN-FREE

MAKES ABOUT 1 CUP · PREP TIME: 5 MINUTES · COOK TIME: 30 MINUTES

2 tablespoons vegan butter

½ cup packed light
   brown sugar

1 tablespoon
   vanilla extract

2 cups unsweetened
   coconut milk from
   a carton

2 teaspoons cornstarch

⅛ teaspoon salt

This creamy sweet sauce is a luscious caramel flavor explosion over any dessert recipe. Try it over Banana Cream Cheese Spring Rolls (page 127). You won't regret it.

1. In a Dutch oven over medium-high heat, stir together the butter and brown sugar, stirring until the brown sugar is completely dissolved, about 1 minute.

2. Turn the heat to low. Add the vanilla. When it starts to bubble, add the coconut milk.

3. Stir in the cornstarch, stirring until the mixture is smooth. Add the salt and stir again.

4. Raise the heat to medium and cook for about 25 minutes, stirring every 5 minutes, until the butterscotch starts to thicken. Remove from the heat and let cool to room temperature. Transfer to an airtight container and refrigerate for up to 2 weeks.

Cooking Tip: When stirring in the cornstarch, make sure to keep the heat low so it easily dissolves without forming any lumps.

PER 1-CUP SERVING: Calories: 792; Total fat: 31g; Sodium: 470mg; Carbohydrates: 157g; Fiber: 2g; Sugars: 110g; Protein: 0g

Jalapeño Mango Chutney

GLUTEN-FREE, NUT-FREE, SOY-FREE, UNDER 30 MINUTES

MAKES ABOUT 2 CUPS • PREP TIME: 5 MINUTES • COOK TIME: 20 MINUTES

1 (1-pound) package frozen mango chunks
¼ cup powdered sugar
2 jalapeño peppers, finely chopped
½ teaspoon ground cumin
¼ teaspoon salt

This is an absolute game-changer recipe. The sweetness of mango when combined with spicy jalapeños is absolutely tantalizing. The chutney tastes best served cold so make big batches to have on hand in your refrigerator at all times.

1. In a stockpot over high heat, stir together the mango, powdered sugar, jalapeño peppers, cumin, and salt. Cook for 4 to 5 minutes until the mango begins to release its juice.

2. Turn the heat to medium-low, cover the pot, and cook for 10 to 12 minutes until heated through.

3. Using a food masher, mash the mixture until it is thick and sticky. Remove from the heat and let cool to room temperature.

4. Transfer to an airtight glass container and refrigerate for up to 1 month.

PER 2-CUP SERVING: Calories: 309; Total fat: 1g; Sodium: 584mg; Carbohydrates: 74g; Fiber: 5g; Sugars: 69g; Protein: 3g

Enchilada Sauce

NUT-FREE, SOY-FREE, UNDER 30 MINUTES

MAKES 1 CUP · PREP TIME: 5 MINUTES · COOK TIME: 20 MINUTES

2 tablespoons olive oil

1 tablespoon minced garlic

**2 tablespoons
all-purpose flour**

1 teaspoon dried oregano

1 teaspoon ground cumin

1 teaspoon chili powder

2 cups vegetable broth

1 tablespoon tomato paste

**1 tablespoon distilled
white vinegar**

½ teaspoon salt

This sauce is quite versatile with its spicy and mild tangy flavor. Enchilada sauce is the key component to a great enchilada recipe and it's also great as a dip for tortilla chips.

1. In a Dutch oven over medium heat, heat the olive oil. Add the garlic and sauté for about 30 seconds until brown. Whisk in the flour and sauté for about 2 minutes until golden.

2. Add the oregano and cumin. Sauté for 1 to 2 minutes until aromatic. Add the chili powder and sauté for 1 minute more.

3. Stir in the vegetable broth, tomato paste, vinegar, and salt. Cover the pot and cook for 5 minutes.

4. Turn the heat to medium-low and stir. Re-cover the pot and cook for 10 minutes more until the sauce thickens. Let cool. Transfer to an airtight container and refrigerate for up to 1 week.

PER 1-CUP SERVING: Calories: 367; Total fat: 29g; Sodium: 2,383mg; Carbohydrates: 26g; Fiber: 5g; Sugars: 6g; Protein: 4g

Onion Mushroom Gravy

NUT-FREE

SERVES 4 · PREP TIME: 10 MINUTES · COOK TIME: 35 MINUTES

2 tablespoons olive oil

1 tablespoon minced garlic

1 teaspoon dried thyme

1 cup chopped onion

8 ounces sliced baby bella mushrooms

2 tablespoons all-purpose flour

2½ cups vegetable broth

2 tablespoons low-sodium soy sauce

½ teaspoon salt

1 teaspoon freshly ground black pepper

Every home cook needs a reliable gravy and you'll use this one all the time.

1. In a skillet over high heat, heat the olive oil. Add the garlic and thyme and cook for about 10 seconds until the garlic starts to brown. Add the onion and sauté for about 2 minutes until brown.

2. Turn the heat to medium and add the mushrooms. Cover the skillet and cook for about 10 minutes until the mushrooms start to brown.

3. Stir in the flour until crumbly, about 1 minute.

4. Stir in the vegetable broth, soy sauce, salt, and pepper. Cover the skillet and cook for 10 minutes.

5. Using a spatula, stir again, scraping the bottom of the skillet. Cook for 5 to 10 minutes more until the mixture starts to thicken. Serve hot.

....

Serving Suggestion: This gravy makes a wonderful topping for Tahini Mashed Cauliflower (page 109).

....

PER SERVING: Calories: 119; Total fat: 7g; Sodium: 1,084mg; Carbohydrates: 12g; Fiber: 3g; Sugars: 4g; Protein: 3g

Lemon Garlic Butter Sauce

GLUTEN-FREE, NUT-FREE, UNDER 30 MINUTES

MAKES ¼ CUP · PREP TIME: 10 MINUTES · COOK TIME: 5 MINUTES

¼ cup vegan butter

2 or 3 garlic cloves, crushed

1 tablespoon freshly squeezed lemon juice

2 teaspoons grated lemon zest

This flavored butter is aromatic and quick to make. Made with vegan butter and flavored with fresh garlic and lemon, your vegetables will be improved with a drizzle.

1. In a Dutch oven over high heat, stir together the butter, garlic, lemon juice, and lemon zest. Cook for 1 to 2 minutes, stirring continuously, until the butter is melted.

2. Turn the heat to low and cook for 30 seconds to 1 minute more, stirring, until aromatic.

3. Let cool to room temperature and transfer to an airtight container. Refrigerate for up to 1 week.

Serving Suggestion: This zesty sauce tastes wonderful drizzled over Paprika Sweet Potato Fries (page 104) or Sautéed Butternut Squash (page 116).

PER SERVING: Calories: 414; Total fat: 44g; Sodium: 485mg; Carbohydrates: 4g; Fiber: 1g; Sugars: 1g; Protein: 1g

Hot Corn Dip

UNDER 30 MINUTES

MAKES ABOUT 2 CUPS · PREP TIME: 10 MINUTES · COOK TIME: 15 MINUTES

2 tablespoons olive oil

1 teaspoon dried garlic

1 tablespoon all-purpose flour

½ cup unsweetened coconut milk from a carton

1 (8-ounce) package vegan cream cheese

2 tablespoons nutritional yeast

1 jalapeño pepper, finely chopped

1 teaspoon freshly ground black pepper

3 cups frozen corn

Salt

Ready in next to no time, this cheesy spicy corn dip is perfect for chips, crackers, and veggies, too.

1. In a Dutch oven over high heat, heat the olive oil.

2. Turn the heat to medium. Add the garlic and flour and sauté for 1 minute.

3. Whisk in the coconut milk and cook for about 30 seconds until the mixture starts to thicken.

4. Stir in the cream cheese, nutritional yeast, jalapeño pepper, and black pepper, stirring until completely combined.

5. Stir in the corn. Cover the pot and cook for about 10 minutes until the corn is tender.

6. Stir the mixture to combine completely, taste and season with salt, and serve hot. Refrigerate any leftovers in an airtight container for up 3 to 4 weeks.

Cooking Tip: Wear gloves while handling the jalapeño to avoid the oil coming in contact with your skin.

PER ½-CUP SERVING: Calories: 390; Total fat: 23g; Sodium: 231mg; Carbohydrates: 41g; Fiber: 4g; Sugars: 7g; Protein: 12g

Béchamel Sauce

SOY-FREE, UNDER 30 MINUTES

MAKES 2 CUPS · PREP TIME: 5 MINUTES · COOK TIME: 20 MINUTES

2 tablespoons olive oil

2 tablespoons all-purpose flour

2½ cups unsweetened coconut milk from a carton

1 teaspoon salt

1 teaspoon freshly ground black pepper

Béchamel is a basic cream sauce that is a staple of French and Italian cuisines. Though traditionally made with dairy milk and butter, it is easily veganized by replacing those ingredients with plant-based milk and oil. Use this as a sauce on its own, such as over pasta, or as a mother sauce for more complex concoctions.

1. Heat a stockpot over high heat.

2. Turn the heat to medium-low. Add the olive oil and flour and sauté for about 3 minutes until the flour is aromatic. Do not let the flour brown.

3. Stir in the coconut milk, salt, and pepper. Raise the heat to medium, cover the pot, and cook for 10 minutes. Stir. Cook for about 5 minutes more until the sauce thickens a bit.

4. Refrigerate any leftovers in an airtight container for up to 2 weeks.

Cooking Tip: Béchamel can be used in any dish that calls for a white sauce, like lasagna, gratin, scalloped potatoes, or macaroni and cheese.

PER ½-CUP SERVING: Calories: 102; Total fat: 10g; Sodium: 591mg; Carbohydrates: 4g; Fiber: 1g; Sugars: 1g; Protein: <1g

Hot Spinach Dip

GLUTEN-FREE, UNDER 30 MINUTES

MAKES 1 CUP · PREP TIME: 5 MINUTES · COOK TIME: 20 MINUTES

1 tablespoon olive oil

8 ounces vegan
　cream cheese

2 tablespoons
　unsweetened coconut
　milk from a carton

1 teaspoon dried garlic

2 tablespoons
　nutritional yeast

½ teaspoon salt

1 teaspoon freshly ground
　black pepper

6 ounces fresh
　baby spinach

Traditional spinach dip is loaded with dairy. When you replace the dairy with coconut milk and vegan cream cheese, as you do here, you get this wonderful recipe everyone will love.

1. In a skillet over high heat, heat the olive oil. Add the cream cheese, coconut milk, and garlic. Cook for about 1 minute, stirring, until the cream cheese melts.

2. Turn the heat to medium. Stir in the nutritional yeast, salt, and pepper.

3. Add the spinach and stir to combine. Cover the skillet and cook for about 10 minutes until the spinach wilts. Stir. Cook for 5 minutes more and serve immediately. Refrigerate any leftovers in an airtight container for up to 2 weeks.

PER ½-CUP SERVING: Calories: 475; Total fat: 36g; Sodium: 1,094mg; Carbohydrates: 23g; Fiber: 4g; Sugars: 4g; Protein: 18g

Arrabbiata Sauce

GLUTEN-FREE, NUT-FREE, SOY-FREE, UNDER 30 MINUTES

MAKES 1 CUP • PREP TIME: 5 MINUTES • COOK TIME: 25 MINUTES

2 tablespoons olive oil

1 tablespoon minced garlic

3 cups finely chopped tomato

1 tablespoon tomato paste

2 teaspoons red pepper flakes

1 teaspoon salt

1 teaspoon freshly ground black pepper

2 tablespoons chopped fresh basil

Slightly different from marinara sauce, arrabbiata has the concentrated flavor of tomatoes cooked in olive oil and a spicy kick from red pepper flakes. Fresh basil adds a hint of brightness and a subtle aroma.

1. In a skillet over high heat, heat the olive oil. Add the garlic and sauté for about 10 seconds until brown.

2. Stir in the tomato, tomato paste, red pepper flakes, salt, and black pepper. Turn the heat to medium. Cover the skillet and cook for 15 to 20 minutes until the sauce reduces slightly.

3. Mix well, scraping the bottom of the skillet. Add ¼ cup water and bring to a boil.

4. Stir in the basil and serve as desired.

PER ½-CUP SERVING: Calories: 192; Total fat: 15g; Sodium: 1,188mg; Carbohydrates: 16g; Fiber: 3g; Sugars: 7g; Protein: 3g

Measurement Conversions

VOLUME EQUIVALENTS (LIQUID)

US STANDARD	US STANDARD (OUNCES)	METRIC (APPROXIMATE)
2 tablespoons	1 fl. oz.	30 mL
¼ cup	2 fl. oz.	60 mL
½ cup	4 fl. oz.	120 mL
1 cup	8 fl. oz.	240 mL
1½ cups	12 fl. oz.	355 mL
2 cups or 1 pint	16 fl. oz.	475 mL
4 cups or 1 quart	32 fl. oz.	1 L
1 gallon	128 fl. oz.	4 L

OVEN TEMPERATURES

FAHRENHEIT	CELSIUS (APPROXIMATE)
250°F	120°C
300°F	150°C
325°F	165°C
350°F	180°C
375°F	190°C
400°F	200°C
425°F	220°C
450°F	230°C

VOLUME EQUIVALENTS (DRY)

US STANDARD	METRIC (APPROXIMATE)
⅛ teaspoon	0.5 mL
¼ teaspoon	1 mL
½ teaspoon	2 mL
¾ teaspoon	4 mL
1 teaspoon	5 mL
1 tablespoon	15 mL
¼ cup	59 mL
⅓ cup	79 mL
½ cup	118 mL
⅔ cup	156 mL
¾ cup	177 mL
1 cup	235 mL
2 cups or 1 pint	475 mL
3 cups	700 mL
4 cups or 1 quart	1 L

WEIGHT EQUIVALENTS

US STANDARD	METRIC (APPROXIMATE)
½ ounce	15 g
1 ounce	30 g
2 ounces	60 g
4 ounces	115 g
8 ounces	225 g
12 ounces	340 g
16 ounces or 1 pound	455 g

References

American Institute for Cancer Research. "AICR's Foods That Fight Cancer." http://www.aicr.org/foods-that-fight-cancer.

Slavin, J. L. "Dietary Fiber and Body Weight." Nutrition 21, no. 3 (March 2005): 411–8. doi:10.1016/j.nut.2004.08.018.

Tuso, P. J., M. H. Ismail, B. P. Ha, and C. Bartolotto. "Nutritional Update for Physicians: Plant-Based Diets." *Permanente Journal* 17, no. 2 (Spring 2013): 61–66. doi:10.7812/TPP/12-085.

U.S. Departments of Agriculture and Health & Human Services. *2015–2020 Dietary Guidelines for Americans.* January 2016. http://www.health.gov /dietaryguidelines/2015.

Index

Acknowledgments

First of all, I would like to thank my mom for sharing her cooking tips and secrets with me. It is because of her that I discovered myself and my passion for cooking.

Secondly, my husband has played a very important role in my career. He encouraged me throughout the process of writing this book, in every respect, from tasting to grocery shopping to babysitting.

Lastly, I would like to thank my very close friends who were always available for taste testing on short notice.

About the Author

Gunjan Dudani is a business analyst turned full-time food blogger and founder of kiipfit.com, a blog dedicated to healthy vegan cooking. Her passion in life is to whip up innovative vegan recipes that are comforting, healthy, easy to make, and, of course, delicious. Her recipes have been featured in *Taste of Home*, *BuzzFeed*, *Greatist*, and *Huffington Post*.

Gunjan was born in Houston, Texas, and now lives in Washington with her two beautiful school-going daughters and loving husband.

CPSIA information can be obtained
at www.ICGtesting.com
Printed in the USA
JSHW041717140420
5087JS00001B/1

9 781646 116560